ABOUT MORNING RUN

"... a small book that goes deep. Deep into the author, but also deep into the reader. In *Morning Run* Harry Pritchett explores the mystery of the unknown within, and discovers grace and life there."

    Loren B. Mead, Executive Director
    The Alban Institute

"... a very moving account of the observations of a creative priest who brings his faith to bear on how he views the world and himself within it. My wife and I found once we began this remarkable diary, we couldn't put it down."

    James C. Fenhagen, Dean and President
    The General Theological Seminary

"During his sabbatical in New York City, Harry Pritchett fearlessly opened up his heart and spirit in a unique book. *Morning Run* may lead one to examine one's own life."

    Wilburn C. Campbell

MORNING RUN

Sabbatical Reflections on the Church and the City

Harry H. Pritchett, Jr.

SUSAN
HUNTER
Publishing
Atlanta

copyright © 1989 by Harry H. Pritchett, Jr.

All rights reserved, including the right to reproduce in whole or part in any form.

Published by Susan Hunter Publishing, Atlanta, Georgia

Manufactured in the United States of America
5 4 3 2 1
Publisher: Susan Hunter
Editor: Phyllis Mueller
Editorial Assistant: Nancy Kahnt
Illustrations: Geo Sipp
Author Photo: Susan Hunter

Permission requested to quote from *Into the Woods* by Stephen Sondheim, from Warner/Chappell Music, Inc., 9000 Sunset Blvd., Penthouse, Los Angeles, CA. 90069-1819.

Permission to quote from *The Power of Myth* by Joseph Campbell with Bill Moyers, 1988, was granted by Doubleday, Bantam Doubleday Dell Publishing Group, Inc., 666 Fifth Avenue, New York, New York 10103.

Library of Congress Cataloging-in-Publication Data

Pritchett, Harry H., 1935–
    Morning run: sabbatical reflections on the church and the city / by Harry H. Pritchett, Jr.
        p. cm.
    ISBN 0-932419-26-7 : $8.95
    1. Pritchett, Harry H., 1935– . 2. Episcopal Church—Clergy—Biography. 3. Anglican Communion—United States—Clergy—Biography. 4. New York (N.Y.)—Description—1981– 5. City churches—United States. I. Title.
BX5995.P74 1989
283′.092—dc20
[B]   89-28745
                                                                          CIP

For Allison

CONTENTS

1
September

27
October

67
November

INTRODUCTION

These morning musings were intended for me and, perhaps, for God, but for no one else. At the time I wrote them, it never occurred to me that anyone would ever see them. So even though they are shortened by half, censored, and edited extensively, I am still somewhat reluctant and even embarrassed that others glimpse snapshots of the landscape of my soul. I hope that the reader will simply consider them a personal sharing of episodic reflections, an extended prayer concerning myself, the city of New York, the world as I see it, and the Divine among us all. If this is so, then I am comforted and feel my purpose in publishing has been achieved.

  The outward facts which are nowhere recorded in what follows are these: I am the rector of All Saints' Church, a large Episcopal parish in downtown Atlanta. During the fall of 1988 I was privileged to take a three-month sabbatical in New York City. The choice of living in New York seemed peculiar to some, and the program I developed for myself seemed even more strange. With the express purpose of living outside official church responsibilities or connections, and exploring what I came to call "covert," as opposed to "overt" theology, I took classes in art history, painting, movie-making, and theater. I read some explicit theology at General Seminary and I thank Dean Fenhagen and others on his staff for their hospitality. But mostly I reflected upon and observed life in the city and my reaction to it.

  When I returned to All Saints', I offered a short lecture series on church and city issues, and in preparing for these lectures, I decided to use a few excerpts from my journal. The reaction to this reading was profound and extensive, so much so that I continued the series, by almost totally reading from the journal. Many people requested that it be published, and what follows is a result of their urgings, as well as the graciousness of Sue Hunter, my publisher.

Other information: I've been married for thirty-three years to Allison, my lover and best friend, who appears with little explanation on these pages. Our children are Sonny, who is thirty-two and a banker; Margaret, who is thirty and working on her Ph.D. in education; and Doug, who is twenty-five and a musician in a rock band. First names of friends and acquaintances are generally used and little attempt has been made to disguise identities. I have added brief identifications for clarity.

Our fourth floor, walk-up apartment was located on Fulton Street in lower Manhattan across from the South Street Seaport and St. Margaret House, a high-rise residential project for the elderly, sponsored by Trinity Church. The first floor consists of commercial shops; the second and third floors are used by the Sisters of St. Margaret who exercise their ministry across the street. Also on the third floor lives the director of social services of St. Margaret's and his wife. This sabbatical experience would not have been possible without the generous gift of lodging there by the Reverend Dan Matthews, Rector of Trinity Church, and to him and to Trinity Church I will be forever indebted.

One final disclaimer: these reflections are just that—reflections—momentary snatches of thoughts scribbled quickly in a notebook. Even though edited from the original, these lines are not reasoned positions or thoughtful essays. As I read back over this material, I realize some of my opinions have changed over the months, but because it is a journal, I have chosen to maintain the initial expressions.

I am most grateful to the clergy staff of All Saints' Church: Barbara, John, David, and Martha, who did far more than keep things going while I was gone, and to all the parish staff who are true colleagues in our ministry together. Most especially I am beholden to Donna Tabaka, who diligently typed these reflections with infinite patience, skill, and good cheer.

But most of all, I want to thank the people of All Saints' Church, without whom, for me, the Holy Catholic Church simply would not exist. They are my run, and they are my morning.

SEPTEMBER

September

WEDNESDAY

What makes Harry run? I'm 52 years old, and I'm not really sure what drives me. Maybe that's the question for my sabbatical reflections. What is it that motivates me—that drives me—that fires my engine? Is it curiosity? Maybe. Is it ambition? Perhaps. Is it power? Maybe. Is it greed? Not really. Is it compassion? On occasion. Is it faith? More than I readily admit. There's something about always wanting to do and be and try something different and new that pushes me around and calls me forward and keeps me running.

But what is it that makes me actually run; I mean run, like hitting the street with my feet and taking off? It's definitely not just concern for my physical health, even though I began for that reason. It's not even primarily for my soul's health. Running is a rather sensual thing for me. It *feels* good, even when it's bad or even when it hurts. I know I'm alive.

When I run I live into the illusion that I'm really in charge—that I'm in control of my life. And for this 45 minutes, 3 or 4 mornings a week, I am.

Well, not really. But it seems this way. In pure fact I could drop dead any minute or be murdered or mugged and that's why I'm careful and I carry an identification card all the time.

Yet this very morning, even in the strange territory of New York City, I felt in charge of my destiny.

On the other hand, this morning's run, which was my first in the Big Apple, was very, very tentative. I didn't go far. It's been only an hour since I stopped and it's difficult to remember where I went. I remember only the lingering smell of the Fulton Street fish market and the hard impression of concrete up and down and under me everywhere. Did I even see one patch of green? I don't think so. This is definitely not Kansas, Toto. It's not even midtown Atlanta!

Morning Run

But God, do I love the mornings, all the mornings. "New every morning in thy love," the old hymn sings, joining the psalmist and me in "taking the wings of the morning." After all, morning is resurrection time! New beginnings reveal themselves as the pink hits the pavement.

It occurred to me today that the main thing I will miss when I die is the morning. Or maybe all "time" will be morning there. That's it! Heaven will be perpetual morning! That's a lot better image than "golden streets and pearly gates" even though I always tend to picture them in "dawn's early light."

Meanwhile, back on earth, here I am. Rather, here Allison and I are. The sun has now completely come up. It's day. Early day of our first day in the city.

We arrived yesterday at about 2 p.m. It was a long trip up, visiting with Harold and Virginia, our old friends in Charlottesville, and spending the night at Doug's new house in Arlington. Sonny drove to New York from D.C. with us. We were glad to have his company, and also his help in unloading all our stuff and carrying it up to the fourth floor.

I'm feeling terribly ambiguous about getting away and about being here. I'm excited, but scared. I'm not sure of what... no structure? No role? Is this the slow-burn anti-structure that Victor Turner writes about, where roles are confused? Can I be a student? Can I relax? Can I exist without power? I seem to want to be in a different role, not a clergy role. My shaggy hair symbolizes that. Perhaps, another role. But I am scared of no role.

The apartment surpasses all our expectations—so open, large. We rearrange furniture, to make the space our space. We think it looks better. It feels more "ours."

God, the people here! Everywhere. Where did they all come from? Tonight it will be less populated when everybody goes home, but this afternoon I was astounded at the sheer number of folk.

September

I think of how little and insignificant it makes me feel to be one of so many. Could God love each one... *each* one? Does anything "beyond" here and now *matter* to them—each of *them*? Each one is different—each one afraid—each one gifted—each one with a different story, different wants, different desires, everything... ah, what mystery.

And each one will die! Each will die alone. Could there really be anything "later" or "beyond" for each of them? For me?

Numbers, numbers, countless skyscrapers, so many overwhelm me. I want a small space; I want my space. It is interesting that within hours of arriving, Allison and I are rearranging, making the space ours, giving us specialness in the masses. Is our uniqueness only an illusion? Oh, Jesus... do you... are you... will you?

THURSDAY

Today I see dirt and filth. This city is absolutely filthy, the buildings decaying, the streets needing repair. I drove all over the Village, the East Village, Chinatown, Little Italy today. God, everything is so broken down; there's graffiti on every wall!

How did it get this way? I keep thinking of how it must have been in the past, when it was new—all clean and fresh—the parks nice and green. Most of the parks are filled with homeless folk now, or shut down, or overgrown. What is our country coming to? Is New York simply not fixable, not governable? Are there too many people, too poor to do anything, here? There are no shiny, vigorous streets and buildings nearby. They're always far away. There's nothing that conveys brassy America—gutsy, adolescent America—daring in vision, like the mere presence of the Brooklyn Bridge must have "said" when it was built a hundred years ago. There is no aged patina of elegance anywhere either. Everything looks filthy, broken down, and worn out.

Morning Run

Are we all ultimately coming to that? Everything filthy, broken down, and worn out? I remember the apocalyptic scenes of the future in *A Clockwork Orange*. Maybe those images are not our future, but our now!

Questions are easier to write than answers. There are no answers for me. And asking the questions somehow relaxes me. The German mystic, Rilke, advised, "Live the questions!" Well I'm doing it! It's 1:30 in the morning and I cannot sleep. Too much stimulation. I need routine. Routine is a blessing. It is needed structure. It helps get me "through the night," as well as through my life.

FRIDAY

If Wednesday's theme was "so many people" and yesterday's was "dirt and decay," today's is violence.

After an absolutely sleepless night, I decided to look for a place that could repair the VCR which I stupidly had left in the trunk of the car. I went down to where the car was parked on the street, and, bingo: lock broken, radio-tape deck gone, VCR gone; even the battery had been disconnected in an attempt to steal!

I feel violated, angry, and a victim. I've had it. Take me back where I know whom to call, where it is comfortable. I feel so alienated. No place to hang my hat emotionally, no home base other than Allison, and she is as disoriented as I am. We really are getting old, I guess. We are homeless, alien. Maybe the one true function of the church in a rootless, violent society, where nobody knows my name, is to give me a name.

Coming up the steps alone, after finding a place uptown where I will take the car to get repaired and then being stopped in a very long traffic jam in Chinatown on the way back, I hear the faint sound of the nuns in their apartment below in corporate prayer. I wait on the stairs, look at my watch. Is it noonday

September

prayers? No. It's only 11:30. They finish, and a deep, unaccented, mellow sound of one of them continues. I can't make out all the words—just a few. "Only boast in your mercy," I hear.

I feel comforted in this alien, violent place. Soft waves of solace roll over me. No absolutes, just the quiet and soft comfort of the familiar from the past makes me satisfied in my forlornness. Yes, satisfied and forlorn at the same time. "Only boast in your mercy." I breathe deeply as I continue up to the fourth floor.

SATURDAY

My Saturday morning run was wonderfully quiet and awesome, all the way around the World Trade Center Plaza and both towers, down by Trinity Church, Battery Park, back around to the Seaport. The sun coming up in the cool day over the Brooklyn Bridge... what a sight. The magnificence of nature (in the sun) and the equal magnificence of man (in the Bridge) combine in a sort of incarnation spirit... nature-man, creator and co-creator. I bought the *New York Times* and literally glowed to fresh coffee and all the pages. Thanks. Thanks. There has to be somebody to thank for the morning!

Yesterday afternoon's activities—going on the subway, looking around The New School, walking around Broadway, a drink at the Marriott—all made me feel more familiar, more at home. I walked by the nuns' apartment again, hearing the muted voices say familiar, almost indistinguishable words. They are from the Apostles' Creed. "I believe." Do I? The sound of the Creed is comforting. It brings a peculiar solace again.

Learning to negotiate the subway system is like learning another language. Until one does, one is isolated and alien in a foreign land. Just making two short trips yesterday helped me. I'm beginning to "speak" subway, very haltingly, but at least I'm making needed contact with this underground labyrinthine animal. Sitting on a subway, looking at people, I ask again, can each one matter? Really matter? Like ants in an anthill, is each really an individual with a soul? What a mystery! Can the church address that mystery?

SUNDAY

So many things yesterday. Our first theater of the trip, in the new Marquis Theater in Portman's Marriott hotel. Jim Dale was wonderful in *Me and My Girl*. It was frothy. It was beautiful. We went on "two-fer" tickets from TKTS. A nice afternoon.

I realize I still feel so much more at home on the upper east side and in midtown. That's where I've been in the past. The people look "nice" there—they are my type and my class. The streets are clean and not so noisy as Fulton Street. What amazes me is how comforting that is in the middle of my anxiety and alienation down where we live. Maybe a lesson about snobbery, or sticking with your own kind.

Class structure grows out of fear—being alienated, uncomfortable in a new setting. That's why it's so bad, so present, so ghetto-ized in the city, and not as true in small towns. The alienation and the loneliness and the fear and the anxiety of the city push people together rigidly with their own kind. I can contrast this with how I grew up in Tuscaloosa. Could Verner School, the grammar school I attended, with all its white diversity ever exist in New York City? Of course not. We were so comfortable and cozy and known in small town Alabama in the forties. Diversity was tolerated ... at least within the races. But none of that cozy comfort is present in the city; hence, rigid ghettos.

I am not sleeping. It's such a terrifying thing, totally beyond my control. It ruins my nights, and also my days. It keeps me depressed and sleepy all the time. I'm running on adrenalin, not natural for me. The noise in this apartment is deafening all night. Endless voices,

September

the rap beat of boom boxes, the clang of garbage trucks at 3 a.m. And a general roar all the time. I bought earplugs in the Village the other day, but they don't help much. I don't know what to do. Lord have mercy, Christ have mercy, Lord have mercy!

When we took Sonny to the airport yesterday, I again was overcome by the horrible streets and the potholes and the bumps and the filth and the garbage and the litter everywhere. All along the highway to the airport. Yet along the dirty streets, great bunches of sunflowers grow profusely. Out of and in the cracks in the cement road... profuse... blowing in the breezes made by passing cars and trucks. Dancing, swaying, laughing, brave sunflowers! Ah... Jesus!

MONDAY

Yesterday was bad and got worse. No sleep the night before. Allison and I are growing tired of so much togetherness without a break. My back hurt worse and worse as the day went on. And my throat got sorer and sorer. Maybe, in fact, I'm getting sick. Sonny and Doug both had colds. Maybe I caught one from them.

The sound of the cement trucks working on the building next door is screeching, roaring, and loud! Allison and I have to scream at each other just to hear. We sound angry with each other. What is it that the behaviorists say? Behavior leads to feelings, not vice versa. Maybe it's true. We act and sound angry, and so we get angry.

This morning I feel better, but not well. Why is it? I'm sick with a cold for the first time in years on our first week in New York. Our once-in-a-lifetime trip, and I'm sick. And so is Allison. I guess I'm not a good adjuster. The truth is that both of us are highly sensitive to external change.

At the Seaport, about dusk yesterday, we had a drink and watched the people. Now I notice not only

Morning Run

how many people there are, but how ugly they all look. Or at least most of them. Finding an attractive person is hard to do! Most look ugly and unhappy. The younger they are, the happier they look. Like puppies. Do you ever see an ugly, unhappy puppy? No. They're all cute and cuddly. But plenty of ugly dogs with sad eyes. The same with people.

What does life do to us? What do we do with life? We don't seem to be equipped to handle what Hamlet calls "the slings and arrows of outrageous fortune." Ugly and sad eyes.

Also, Allison and I tend to notice more the Japanese and the middle-easterners. We are rather startled and ultimately laugh about our inescapable racism. Can we ever be rid of it? God help us not to act on it.

We saw an exhibition at the Whitney Museum downtown on "Words in Art." It was ostentatious, boring, and an artistic put on. Just "pictures" of words or paragraphs or letters alone. Maybe I'm just older, but I can't understand this sort of elitist, taking-one's-self-too-seriously kind of thing. Either New York is too sophisticated or I'm too red-necked.

TUESDAY

I met Jimmy at St. Margaret's House today. He's one of the sextons. Also I met Sisters Arlen and Eleanora, two of the nuns who live below us and work at St. Margaret's. There was something about knowing their names that soothed my sense of being alien. People are nice individually, somehow.

We took a subway to the Museum of Modern Art. In spite of the cold that I caught from Sonny and Doug, I was impressed. It is nice to take one's time in a museum, and not feel hurried or rushed. So we didn't get through. Who cares? I'm particularly aware of the alienated non-human images in modern art. They are abstract with straight lines. Very few curves, no human curves.

September

Of course there's an absence of religious symbols, except Chagall. They are almost comic and unintentional in Chagall. Like Chagall's figures, perhaps we are not "grounded"... just floating, along and alone, in the air.

What anti-structure! I want to discover more about me and us, out of role, out of the structure of the church. Will I just float away like a Chagall figure? Who knows? But today I don't feel very floating with this cold. Rather, I feel like I'm heavy and sinking. I bought an *Atlanta Constitution* on 42nd Street today. It is good to read of home and the familiar. I notice Allison read the *Constitution* whereas she has not read the *New York Times*.

We are to go tomorrow night to Bill and Nell Martin's apartment. He's the business manager at Trinity Church and an old Alabama acquaintance. I look forward to that. There is comfort in the anticipation of being with people who are friends of people we know, who will at least know our names.

WEDNESDAY

Early this morning, as I turned the corner at the Seaport, the red sun was rising over the Brooklyn Bridge. What a sight! I said out loud, "Thank you!" It was magnificent. Moving on down Water Street to Battery Park was exhilarating. Saw other runners in the park.

The city is becoming friendlier, I think. Even so, I still feel like a visitor.

A beautiful day. We took the car uptown to be repaired and left it. Allison and I walked and rode the bus twice to get back home. We sat for a long time in Washington Square in the sunshine, watching the people. Very nice and easy. I'm beginning to feel more at home in the city. People speak to us more. I'm not as cool as people say we should be. Allison has conversations on the bus and elsewhere. Casual conversation

Morning Run

comes so easily for her. Mere strangers sense a comfort and no judgment in her manner. It is really true: everybody, well almost everybody, loves Allison. And so do I.

Sitting in Washington Square at lunch with thousands of people, I noticed the crosses on top of churches around the Square. Do these folks think of Jesus as a reality? Is the totally secular city which Harvey Cox describes really true? Is there no mystery for most? Does any of it matter? Is the cross an empty symbol?

THURSDAY

Mother called this morning to say that Ann Holifield had died. As I write this, it seems incredible. People who are our age, people we have known all our lives, people we went to birthday parties with as children, people who are godparents to our children are not supposed to die! But she did. I feel grief and I feel fear. Allison and I both cried after talking with Stan, her husband.

Maybe that's another role for the church. What do people in the anonymous city do with death? Who is there? Perhaps this is the role of the community, but it's more than just secular community. Death puts everything into a more eternal, mystical realm. Is there anything "beyond"? Anything? Anybody?

I find the Prayer Book burial service deficient. It uses a lot of images that seem to me to be extremely empty in our world. It needs simplifying. In death everything needs to be simple. Simply said, sung, and stated. It is not a time for involved, complicated images or concepts like "resurrection of the body" or "the consummation of all things."

Sister Coreta had a point when she said that to believe in God is to have the great faith that somewhere, someone is not stupid. She also said to believe in God is to be willing to die and not be embarrassed.

September

Hallelujah! To not believe in God is to accept the obvious. That no one, anywhere has any sense about things, or people, or me. And that is very embarrassing, indeed.

The nuns were singing today as I passed the door. What is it about their persistence, their discipline, their simplicity that attracts me so? I dare to stop in the hall—eavesdropping on their worship, being cheered from afar—outside the door by the routine of the tradition.

FRIDAY

A wonderful run this morning all through Battery Park and the World Trade Center Plaza with the sun rising, down to the water, seeing the Statue of Liberty which looks so little from the park.

Les Miserables last night was long, but splendid and grand and noble in purpose. Yet somehow it lacked juice for me, and it was bad liturgy. The audience wasn't given time to participate, not enough pauses or reprises. Yet it was cleverly staged and lighted. In fact, the set was the star.

It puzzles me that an opera like this, so heavy handed, is terribly popular. What is it? The theme of freedom? Something about being overwhelmed with big, spectacular sets? I don't know, but it does not overwhelm me emotionally. There's something fundamentally ironic in paying fifty dollars a ticket to be moved by a show about the poor, the miserable. Perhaps it is we who are *les miserables*, and we don't even know it.

We rode the bus home at midnight—three busses, in fact, before we made it all the way down the island. Bus drivers were accommodating and helpful, telling us what to do. We must get over being afraid, particularly Allison. It's amazing how stories about New York's violence have influenced us and keep us estranged from

Morning Run

the city. We need to be cautious, but not stagnated by fear.

I bought a bunch of daisies yesterday. They are so fresh and clean still this morning. I bought them for Allison in memory of Ann. Her funeral was yesterday. I still can't believe she's dead, really gone. It's all over.

The sun is blazing in through these four big windows in our apartment. What a sunny room! Bright light bathing the daisies. Daisies in the concrete.

A slow life is very appealing. I must learn to live it and feel okay about me. I must learn that it is not necessary to accomplish something all the time in order to avoid despair. Death takes us all, and illusions of immortality by accomplishment are a sin. Good Lord, deliver us. Good Lord, deliver me!

SATURDAY

I'm trying to be disciplined about writing in the morning. It seems the best time, but this means reflections are always on yesterday, digested overnight by dreams and my increasing lack of memory.

Anyway, it still seems the most logical time for writing and running. The end of the day is too unpredictable. I never know what I'll be doing or what will be going on.

Like birth and death. Birth is much more "regular," predictable, dependably "on time." Death is anytime, unpredictable, yet finally dependable.

Anyway, all entries are yesterdays. And yesterday was beautiful—clear and crisp air. Deceptively clean. I made my first venture alone in the subway, all the way to Fiftieth Street with one transfer to pick up the car. Unbelievable bill of $950. Along with buying another VCR, the little incident of theft last Friday night cost $1200.

Damn!

September

Again, *Me and My Girl* last night from the orchestra thanks to All Saints' friends, Reg and Sis. It is a purely delightful show. Better to be up close, where the audience perceives an energy on stage and identifies with the characters in the play. Somehow, mysteriously, we had an illusion of being together, members of instant community. ("Did you see that?" "Wasn't it wonderful?" "I felt moved." We all were moved.) Through the characters in the play we, for the moment, become one. A mystery.

That seems to say something about momentary community and liturgy. I sometimes wonder if that sort of thing happens during the services at All Saints'. People identify with and feel affection for the staff who is "up front" leading the liturgy. And they experience us as liking each other, which in fact we do. And somehow that gives a feel of unity and community. Even though, of course, it is lacking in substance over the long haul. It's a temporary thing, valid but only for the moment. The trouble is that the long-term expectation of belonging in more intimate fashion, then, may not be met. Sunday visitors at All Saints' tell me they experience warmth; some even use the word energy. While not denying the reality of momentary, liturgical community, how can or does that translate into real community? Perhaps it doesn't. Maybe liturgical community is enough.

Allison and I sometimes get on each other's nerves spending so much time together, even in New York with all there is to do and so much space in this large apartment. Our covenant of intimacy is sometimes strained. Just imagine how it is with most families or couples or friends living in far less space in the city. No wonder there is violence. How can it be avoided? Some vital community other than the family is absolutely necessary. Providing that community could be an essential role for the church in the city.

Morning Run

SUNDAY

Yesterday was a wonderful trip to the Village to an art show all around Washington Square and NYU. Actually, more things (bracelets, jewelry, clothes, horoscopes, chiropractic consultations, palm-readings) for sale than art. A little art, not very exciting. It reminded me of Atlanta's Piedmont Arts Festival, but not as interesting. The people were *more* interesting. The people always are. This was our second long sitting in Washington Square. But today the crowd was even more heterogeneous—all shapes and sizes. A young man handed me a leaflet saying, "Learn about complete salvation in Jesus Christ." I took it and said, "I have." He said, "Have you experienced it?" I said, "Yes," smiled, and kept walking. I thought to myself, "You mean, have I experienced it the way you have?"

We took a long ride around Manhattan. Allison is terrified of my driving. I think my driving is just fine. I get around better when she's not there trying to navigate. I tell her this. She cries. Most of the rest of the drive she's silent. I resent her telling me things I already know. It's funny; she doesn't do that as much with the children as she used to. But she's worse about it with me. By evening, however, she is okay. And I am too. A good dinner of fresh salmon, bought at the market. And early to bed.

This morning is overcast. Sunday morning is so quiet by comparison with the rest of the week and Saturday night. Long, slow morning with the *New York Times* and coffee and breakfast. We are going to Trinity Church at 11:15 and then lunch at the church with the Martins, and to the Moscow Circus.

I'm feeling much more at home, not as alien or anxious. Now I'm afraid Allison will always be anxious about being here, and will want me with her all the time. That's not like her, and yet it is like her. She holds the ambiguity of extreme strength and extreme

September

helplessness—independence and dependence. Ah, we are all unfathomable mysteries to ourselves and to others.

MONDAY

Yesterday was Trinity Church and the Moscow Circus at Radio City Music Hall! It was a wonderful day!

I felt peculiarly nervous about going to church. I still don't know why. Allison and I dressed and walked. What a magnificent edifice Trinity Church is! There was a fair-sized crowd. It's hard to say how many people, since the church is so wide that the distance from the back door to the altar doesn't seem very far. Very heterogeneous—black, yellow, old, young, blue jeans and t-shirts, and suits. I didn't see any high-powered Wall Street types. I was told later that only seven people on the vestry are also members of the church.

Somehow, it seemed like a parable of the Kingdom: that glorious architecture and all that music and choreography and pomp and richness for this very ragtag little crowd of simple folk. I loved it and began to feel more connected with these church people. It was as though these strangers held a place for me.

Later on, the Moscow Circus with Nell and Bill Martin was thoroughly entertaining. It was a different sort of secular liturgy, more like a ballet rather than Ringling Brothers' pizzazz. The Martins were easy to be with, genuine and warm, made us feel welcome in the city. We were all like kids watching the circus, particularly the ferocious beauty of the tigers going through the choreography with their trainer. We had a late dinner in Chinatown (Nell had whole frogs!) and then walked home for the first time at night. Peculiarly, I felt so confident and powerful that I knew my way home. We made it safe and sound.

Morning Run

WEDNESDAY

Well, my resolve to write every morning didn't work! I didn't write yesterday. Perhaps it was because yesterday was a nothing day. We did absolutely nothing! I get restless when I don't have at least one thing to do every day.

I went for long walks, however. I took a particularly quieting walk at dusk. I saw the moon rising, the lights on the bridges, and Brooklyn across the river, all hazy like a faded picture. It was absolutely lovely. A delight!

Doug came much later last night after the Grateful Dead concert. He is absolutely lovely, as well. And a delight!

I think some about my children. Will they ever marry? Why? Why not? It's not just one, but all of them. I'm beginning to doubt if they ever will be married. That breaks my heart. What did we do that led them to that? Surely with all three, it's not just chance. There is some dynamic present, but I have no idea what it could be.

It's amazing how the idea of having no grandchildren depresses me. There must be something very, very fundamental in the need for immortality through one's children and one's grandchildren. And it's depressing to think that Allison and I just stop—the end, all over—dust to dust with none of us left over in our offspring's offspring. Can we really be the "grateful dead"? I'm not talking rationally now, nor even out of traditional theology, but from some inchoate, cultural, unconscious feeling.

And today, there has been little to do but meditate on such potential nothingness. It's Sondheim's musical *Into the Woods* tonight, and I look forward to that. Could it be that today's angst comes from the fact that on this trip I'm already into the woods?

September

THURSDAY

Last night *Into the Woods* was so clever, so profound, so endearing. I remember Bettelheim says in *The Uses of Enchantment* that the woods in fairy tales are symbolic of the place where one confronts inner darkness and struggles with identity, and where a person begins again to understand what he or she is called to be. Sondheim uses the woods that way to extremely good effect. Cinderella, Jack (of *Jack and the Beanstalk*), Rapunzel, Little Red Riding Hood, their princes, a baker and his wife, and all the characters take such a journey of self-discovery, conflict, and growth—even the witch! The first act is up-beat and lilting; the second act is reflective, somber, and moving. We were very familiar with the score, having listened to the tape hundreds of times over the last few months. All in all, an exciting, but more than that, a pleasing and thoroughly satisfying evening at the theater.

While I was running this morning, some thoughts from the play crept into my consciousness: fear is the primary obstacle to community. Fear of intimacy—fear of disclosure—fear of truth—fear of change. It is fear that is the opposite of community, nothing else.

This city is law and license, what to do and what not to do, with only small pinches of grace. All the signs say, "Do this and don't do that." They don't say please. (One exception: I noticed a sign at General Seminary which read, "Please Allow the Grass to Grow.") Everything is stern, like the law. The law develops out of fear. License, or just doing your own individual thing regardless of the law, is also fed by fear—fear of any kind of restraint. Law is discipline, and, in fact, is necessary structure and beneficial to the community, but license has no place in the community. Doing what one wants when one wants is an illusion. It's license—it's licentiousness, and denies the truth of Sondheim's theme in *Into the Woods*, no one is alone. No one acts alone. Or

Morning Run

Paul's, "You are the Body of Christ, and individually members of it."

In *Into the Woods*, a statement is made to Little Red Riding Hood to the effect that her mother told her never to stray from the path. To which she replies, "It is the path that has strayed from me." When Jesus said, "I am the way," could it ever be that the way would stray from me?. What blasphemy! Will I be swallowed up, myself, by the Big Bad Wolf?

TUESDAY

Yesterday sort of disappeared. We really did nothing. My big event was riding to Times Square by myself on the subway to get an *Atlanta Constitution*. How nice to just hang out, as the kids would say. But too much of that would drive me crazy. I am defined, to a degree, by my purpose, by what I can do.

Anonymity has its pluses and minuses. I like not being recognized, free to dress and be what I feel like. My long hair is not a rebellion, I think, but an adventure. And yet being anonymous is lonely—at least a bit lonely. I don't know how long I could be anonymous, with no place, no identity.

Homelessness is so prevalent. Homeless people are everywhere on the streets of New York. More than I've ever seen. Homelessness is a state of being—a state of the soul. "My heart is restless 'til it finds itself in thee." Was it Augustine who said that? Maybe it should be changed now to this: "My heart is homeless 'til it finds itself in thee."

Homelessness . . . anonymity . . . loneliness . . .
   these are strange words.
—no place equals Utopia (and homeless).
—no identity equals anonymous (with no name).
—no community equals a lone person (and alone).
but,
I am born alone.

September

I'll die alone.
Ultimately I can only experience the Mystery alone.

We start school today at The New School. I'm rather fearful about it, because I'm a new kid in a new school. But I'm also excited about it, like a kid. I fear the new, even when I'm moving toward connecting with others. I fear that and, peculiarly, I long for that. I want something to do, but more importantly, I want someone to do it with. Now, that's really it. But... but... not *all* of it.

WEDNESDAY

The sisters were in retreat upstate for a week, and I'm glad they're back. This morning about 7 a.m., coming in from my run, I heard the distant, weak and strong voices at prayer, at lessons, and just then, as I was coming up the stairs with my *New York Times*, the faint, high sopranos singing like early sparrows echoing each other across the woods.

It is so, so right! That is no thoughtful, critical assessment. I don't want to be there with them exactly. I like listening from the other side of the door. But I'm glad—happy—pleased—calmed that they do it there. And I know they are praying and they are singing. It is not an anachronism in our times. (Oh, maybe rationally it is. But I'm not speaking rationally. I'm speaking from the heart.)

The first class in Museum Exploring was interesting. Parsons School of Design in midtown was crowded, mostly smart-looking, very young girls. Our small class assembled in a make-shift room, almost a hall. The teacher is a nervous young woman, who seems somewhat scattered and inarticulate. I wonder how she'll be in the Metropolitan Museum?

Yesterday the class went to the Museum of American Crafts on Fifty-seventh Street. The building

Morning Run

is lovely—striking—open. The crafts were interesting: pottery, woven things. I didn't learn anything new, however. There were seven women and me, the only man. That should be interesting as we move along through the course. There's one older woman (seventies?), one smart, new-to-New-York, good-looking woman from the west side, one pregnant girl from the Village, two very young girls from Switzerland here with their men, who are taking courses on Wall Street in international banking. I look forward to knowing these folks better. Allison is already den mother to the group—what a gift she has for building community! It makes me feel a part of things and proud of her. The teacher is scared of me, I think. Could it be my knowledge of art, which is really very meager? Could it be my sex? We shall see.

I really liked the quiet feeling of being at the library at General Seminary yesterday, reading and writing. I will look forward to that sort of discipline every week.

I am also so impressed by Jim, the dean at General Seminary, and his wife Eulalie. We had supper with them last evening. They are so down-to-earth, no frills, straightforward, easy to be with. There is hope for the church when a person like Jim is dean of an important seminary.

THURSDAY

I've been a little melancholy today and last night. I'm not sure why. The Broadway Play class was disappointing. It was made up of typical matinee audience types—Jewish women from all over the suburbs. Most have been in the class for years. My hunch and prejudice is that they are not discriminating theater-goers. The teacher, Dr. Zoe Kaplan, seems interesting, however. She's lively and attempts to bring us new people into the discussion.

September

I'm not sure why I feel so down. Allison is definitely down. She's never gotten into her own program, so to speak, of being here. She admits it. She doesn't know why. Her interests seem suddenly limited, and she seems to have no desire to expand them. She has lost most of her excitement of what we could do when we got here, trips to Maine and Boston. I'm worried about her soul in the dark of night.

When I read about Grein being elected Bishop here in New York, I felt that failure-disappointment thing come over me. It's a feeling of rejection, being excluded from the important people, never-amounting-to-very-much, not being chosen. Why does it haunt me so, creeping up unexpectedly from the dark? Why? Why? Does it really matter? Am I a failure if I'm not a bishop? Of course not, rationally. But this let-down feeling is not rational. It's from some dark corner of my soul, which I don't understand. Maybe it's just that symbol of success that was instilled in me as a little boy. A macho sort of thing. Yet realistically in my life now there are many regrets: doors closing behind me, chances missed, possibilities and options becoming fewer and fewer. However, I do believe that everything that has happened in the past has brought me to this now. There is no going back, except to learn. I am here, now.

Sometimes I'm afraid of being stuck at All Saints' —not good for them or for me. Am I too old for a new project? Well, I can't control the future. Being aware of my feelings is good, however. And I need not make decisions about the future based on rational thought alone! I don't always need to be big and rational and grown up! I will not rule out my feelings. And God, please take all this weird, irrational, crazily-woven-together tapestry of peculiar threads, and re-shape them in some sort of pattern so that your will is done through me—for me—and for your world. Amen.

Morning Run

FRIDAY

Yesterday was full. I was unusually nervous and excited about my first class in oil painting. I felt like a little boy going to a new school. I wanted to appear with-it and cool, but I felt awkward and a little self-conscious.

The classroom was bright and sunny with tall windows and high ceilings on the seventh floor, looking out over the roof tops of Greenwich Village. It met all the romantic notions of my youth of taking an art class in the Village in New York City!

When I arrived, the room was set up with easels in a circle. I chose an easel and tried to look like I knew what I was doing. As I got set up and took out my sketch pad and pencil, I glanced up toward the center of the room, and my eyes caught a glimpse of a large, bare, black breast! The model had arrived and was undressing right there before God and everybody! I tried to maintain my composure and not gawk. Everyone else seemed nonchalant. I continued my cool act. Then the model asked to use my watch. First I couldn't get the damn thing off my arm. I was bumbling and fumbling. And I never was able to tell her how to set it, what with her standing there naked as the day she was born, and me trying to appear sophisticated as the new boy in The New School. My cool act was completely blown. What a scene. I was a slapstick clown!

The teacher is an old, grey-haired man with a kind, worn face. Even though he was articulate and not mushy, he seemed understanding and humble, open to what others were saying. He was easy with me as a beginner, and said I had, "a good, natural eye."

And I do. I observe well. I see more than most, without trying. Maybe it's my obsession with "place"— knowing where I am, where I stand, where I'm coming from. I loved the class, and I did some nice sketches of the model.

Last night was the film class. Loved the teacher; five hundred folks in the class studied *Punchline*. Rich-

September

ard Brown, the teacher, doesn't seem to miss a thing. He had the movie memorized. He pointed out the relationships of scenes to scenes and lines to lines. Under his tutelage, the movie was powerful and moving.

It was amazing that I needed to rest today. I did too much yesterday. Hah! How I've given up stress! I'm really not addicted to it. I dread going back to it. If this was permanent, I would need more limelight and structure, but right now, I love my pace. I may tire of it, but I haven't yet.

This morning was the first brisk taste of fall. Beginning my early run in the dark, I journeyed down to Battery Park, by the water and the Statue of Liberty, around the West Side Highway and up toward the World Trade Center Towers, watching the incredible beauty of the sunrise reflecting gradually on the glass skyscrapers.

As I headed down Fulton Street for a quick circle around St. Margaret's House and the small park, the sun was beginning to light the sky, and suddenly my eyes caught the first red leaf of autumn, on a dogwood tree, I think—by itself, red as blood amidst the fading green leaves on the tree.

Time flies. I think, can it really be fall? Where did the summer go? Almost overnight. And then the phrase appeared to me, as I headed down Water Street on the way back to the apartment, "It is the autumn of your life."

And it is. It really is. I think, autumn is cool and clear with sunny days, a certain mellowness in the air. Vivid colors of yellow and orange and red disguise the increasing dryness and fragility of the leaves, one last burst of excruciatingly beautiful creativity before wrinkling and falling off the winter tree.

I tell myself, you should be getting wiser in the autumn of your life. And yet wisdom seems so distant. I prefer the excesses of spring and the energy of summer. Where is autumn's wisdom?

Morning Run

    And the verse of this hymn comes to me about the time I breathlessly arrive at the newsstand to pick up my *New York Times*, "O come thou wisdom from on high, who orderest all things mightily. To us the path of knowledge show and teach us in her ways to go ... Rejoice, Emmanuel, shall come to you, O Israel!"
    I hummed it going up the steps and through my shower and prayed that the Lord would tolerate an autumn man with a summer heart!

OCTOBER

October

SUNDAY

Yesterday was full. We attended a screening of the movie *Memories of Me* (good acting, bad script). Then Mamet's play, *Speed the Plow* (wordy, not passionate, well written, probably better to read).

The evening with two New York couples that we met at movie class was terrible and so disappointing. Allison and I left the restaurant early. These folks seemed to be so caught up in rich, liberal, "with-itness." And what pretentiousness, which we didn't spot at first. One woman was bitchy; the other maternal. The men played subtle competitive games with a variety of subjects, all of which boiled down to who had the most toys. I thought Allison and I would die of boredom. Allison finally almost went to sleep at the table while they chattered on incessantly, mostly to each other. What is it with folks like them? Our first encounter with true New Yorkers! Are they all form and no substance? Hardly, but we just could not connect. I'm not sure why. Are they typical of eighties chic? Money, power, fame (they know and drop names of the "little" famous people). Where is the juice in the relationships? Where is the softness? Where is even a hint of vulnerability or pain? I couldn't even see it in their eyes.

I long for some shoes-off, easy conversation with people who are not boring, like Harold and Virginia Hallock with whom we visited on the trip up here. They are so comfortable to be with, so caring. They're so interested and interesting! They are not boring. Lately, almost everyone seems boring. I'm not sure if it's just that I was tired and ready to get away, but both Allison and I have found that it is difficult for us to find folk that somehow do not bore us. How utterly arrogant we are.

However, it seems to me that people who don't bore me are (first) open, stretching folk, whose world

Morning Run

view is encompassing, not narrow or narcissistic, and (second) people who are interested in us, our life, our family, genuinely interested. Our life agendas and their life agendas are all important to them; they really listen and really care. And (third) they love us and we love them. That's the best I can do now to define the unboring relationships and/or encounters. I must reflect more on this later. Surely it's not all me.

I don't seem to have reflections of much substance anymore. Why? Am I feeling so at home that things just fly by without reflection? I know I do think and reflect, but I forget when journaling.

My edges are rounding off. Is that dulling me? Making me boring? Or is it maturity? I'm attracted to a mellow quietness, but flashes of pure, hot color are also a part of me. I am red, as well as green.

MONDAY

Yesterday with Steve and Marie, our new, good friends from Atlanta, was fun and definitely not boring! A visit to the Soho loft of an artist friend of theirs was wonderfully typical. And then brunch at One Fifth, a Village restaurant, was charming. Everything yesterday was not frantic and genuine fun. We traveled in a big, black limousine as long as a hearse with telephone, TV, bar and all the works. Last night we had a late dinner with John, a friend from Atlanta who is here on business, at Tavern on the Green. It was touristy with really terrible service, but we were glad to see him and it and to hear about home. We came to our New York home about midnight by cab (he paid), which made us feel real ritzy.

Earlier Allison had gone by herself on the subway to a screening for the movie class. She is moving around again by herself and regaining city confidence in the face of city dislodgement. I went late to church and taught a Sunday school class before we met for lunch.

October

At the Sunday school class, I felt back in my element. I am a gifted teacher. I really communicate with these folks. In the middle of the class it occurred to me I'm doing too well! I'm liking this too much! I move too quickly back to my priestly role.

But I don't miss church. Well yes I do. At least I miss aspects of the community. I like taking the eucharist almost anonymously. I don't need to be up-front. I'm critical of the liturgy and sermons I see and hear, but not overly so.

Being in the new role of not having a role is more comfortable now. Over the long haul, I don't think I'd like it very much, but for now, it is very comfortable.

I'll be glad, happy, excited to get out of the city this weekend. I'm not sure how people stand staying here with no exit possibilities. Space takes on new meaning when, because of the millions of people, individual space is so hard to come by. No wonder people tend toward lonely protectionism, with anger right under the surface all the time. "Don't touch me!" is almost screamed on the street. I notice I don't touch—and even avoid touching others. We pretend on the crowded subway that we are not touching. Body to body we are, but we pretend that we aren't. Can we kill each other from afar without touching? If I touch others, they may invade me, my space. I will be vulnerable to penetration by another. And . . . can we have sex without being touched? God, what a lonely society. At least in the church we touch. We shake hands at Trinity Church at the peace. That's the only touching I know of. But at least there is some sacrament of the "blessed community."

There is so little evidence of community in the city. Perhaps that's what bothered me about the New York couples last week. They were hip people. They seemed to have no need for sloppy, messy, touching, vulnerable community. And maybe they don't.

Morning Run

But I do need it and I miss it. Maybe that's why I feel a mild sort of angst this morning. Somehow, this morning, I need to cry. I have not really been moved much by all the drama we've experienced. I need a powerful catharsis at the theater. I need to be really touched. I need to cry my clogged brain clean. Dear Lord, clean me out. Touch me, clean out my soul with tears.

TUESDAY

Yesterday was so quiet. A wonderful run and couch time with the morning TV. I don't feel as much necessity to read and produce as I did the first weeks. A trip to Times Square for the *Constitution*. I could give that up. It pales so beside the *New York Times*, and the local news in the Sunday edition is minor.

So far, my biggest revelation is the intensity of my ambivalence about the church. On the one hand, there's the almost erotic yearning for it. And on the other hand, a revulsion at the anachronism of it—the arrogance—the pretentious bore of the institution. Maybe the unfolding truth in all of this is that the ambivalence in me is also present in any truly modern person who still longs for home, but knows it's always in the future. Harvey Cox says in *Religion in the Secular City*, that no one can move beyond the secular city who has not first passed through it. I concur. I cannot belong to either polarity. I'm neither the religious ostrich, nor the secular giraffe.

Later, I reflected on early art from my class at the Metropolitan today. Greeks were the first to make realism (looking like the subject, verisimilitude) a criterion for judgment of the worth or beauty of a piece of art. This is not true of Egyptian or Chinese expressions. We judge a work of art "good" when it accurately represents our experience. That assumption is inherited from the Greeks.

October

In all cultures, evidently, representations of people in art begin very stylized and move toward more realistic representations. I wonder why that is? I wonder which is the truest representation of a person, symbolic stylization or photographic realism?

We saw a pre-sixth-century-B.C. Greek urn. Our teacher says that these early urns always were connected with death. She says the dead were eaten. They were sometimes placed in these very large urns (in parts), wine poured over them and drained from the bottom for consumption. One then ate and drank the departed. The kinship with the eucharist is undeniable, even if it seems a little repugnant!

We also talked about sculpture carved from stone, not sculpture constructed and built from clay or metal. The sculptor carves the stone from the outside in, not the inside out. The art of the sculptor is to know where to stop, since one cannot add back the stone already chipped away. The artist must see the statue in the stone before chipping one little bit away. What a miracle!

In Egyptian culture, when one wished to denounce or forget another, one would knock off the nose from the statue of that person so that it could not be animated by the breath of life. However, the worst thing one could do was to scratch off the name, because without a name the afterlife was never available. Without a name, you did not exist. Sometimes people took many names in order never to be without a name and, therefore, nothing, no-thing.

Surely, that will "preach," particularly about baptism. Somehow, some way, the church must declare both with simplicity and straightforwardness: the breath of life is available to animate your stony heart, and within this community you have a name. Your name can never be taken from you. You are... so breathe!

Morning Run

WEDNESDAY

We attended a performance of *Ain't Misbehavin* this afternoon. Some few moments were bright, but the whole thing was not very engaging, just okay.

Is it Broadway, or is it me? Nothing, literally nothing, so far, has been magic. I really want it to be; I hope it will be. But alas, only occasional glimpses—no moments! Everybody on the stage is working hard, but somehow I have not yet entered into the show or the play. I have not been grabbed. I have not been transported, as sometimes in the past. Is it just I who have become jaded? I hope not. I think not.

The Martins are coming over for dinner tonight. Doug is coming for the weekend. We received several calls from home from various folk.

Allison says she is thinking about dropping her design course. I suggest that she talk with her teacher about some of her concerns. (Is it necessary that she buy all the equipment or that she do detailed drawings?) But she says she can't say what she wants to the teacher. She seems to be remarkably conflicted about this. I'm no help to her since I don't understand her conflict. I don't think she really understands what's going on with her either. She lacks grace when she gets into this kind of undifferentiated conflict and she loses interest in outside activities.

Right now she's happy as a lark, fussing around the kitchen, cooking supper for the Martins. But in general she has seemed mildly down lately. I wonder if she could be grieving on some unconscious level her great loss of weight? All of that part of herself that is gone? Grieving for the old self that has passed away? Perhaps. Like any other loss, must it be mourned?

That would be totally irrational, but we humans are simply not rational. She worked so hard to lose almost 80 pounds over the last year. She looks sensational, more beautiful than she has been in twenty

October

years. And nothing has pleased me more! Yet I wonder; that is a lot of "self" to lose, even when one works hard to do it, and no one ever loses any thing easily or without sadness.

There's Nell at the door. I will return to this later.

FRIDAY

Yesterday was a long drive to Maine—ten-and-a-half hours. But it was absolutely beautiful! The leaves were ablaze. Northeastern colors in leaves are just different from down South. Not only are there more leaves (sugar maples and others) but the intensity of the color is stronger and the colors themselves are more varied—oranges, dark maroons, purples, mauves, peaches, dusty roses, taupes.

I wondered—what function do colored leaves play in the ecology, the efficiency of nature? Flowers are functional as well as beautiful. They provide seeds and pollen that is spread by insects attracted to their brilliant color. But what function do colored leaves play? I can think of none. They are simply grace—an extra, a gift, for no reason. They're beauty of and in itself. They are God's extravagance! Surely! God not only looks around at his creation and says, "It is good—it is very good." But also he looks around at things like autumn leaves (and maybe autumn people?) and says, "It is beautiful! They are beautiful!"

We came to Maine to visit the summer house of a friend from Atlanta. Julia's place is right off a picture postcard. The cottage was built in the 1800s—low ceilings because of the cold—wonderfully painted white—situated in the trees along the road with a garden in the back for an acre and a half down to the bay. Oh, what beauty again!

By the way, I forgot to mention the birches—white, stately, straight, accenting the glory of the colored leaves. As the sun went down last evening, they stood

Morning Run

out like ghost trees in the greying dark. Dignified, strong, guarding the profusion of foliage like a picket fence, keeping it in and us out. Oh, the birches. It is all so beautiful. I know I appreciate it more after a month of concrete and noise and dirt and too many people.

How can we retreat in the city? Maybe we cannot. We may need to change our social structures in order to get the poor out of the city sometimes, somewhere. But how? How?

I must not forget, since I didn't write yesterday, to mention the movie class Thursday night on *Madame Sousatzka* with Shirley MacLaine and John Schlesinger (of *Midnight Cowboy, Sunday, Bloody Sunday* and countless other movies). God, what an evening! Both of them are so brilliant and very articulate and very gentle and warm, not Hollywood at all. They were not consumed with themselves. Both seemed to accept and deal gracefully with middle age, the body "turning down," as she called it. Their knowledge of film art was incredible, all from experience. Their insight into people and characters was remarkable. A truly exciting, stimulating evening, from the fourth row no less!

Occasionally I feel overstimulated. Can one have too many stimuli? I can't hold them all, but who cares? Hold them for what? To enjoy, to savor like a delicious meal. To learn what is revealed without working at it!

Oh, the quiet in this New England morning! Thank you! Thank you! Without God, there would be no one to thank for the morning.

MONDAY

Somehow I didn't write the last two days in Maine. Perhaps it was the sheer exuberance of bathing myself in the beauty. It felt like going into another land: the quiet, the countryside, the foliage, the white clapboard architecture. It snowed four inches Saturday night—big,

October

wet, sloppy snowflakes—absolutely stunning on the evergreens. What a feast of color and shapes, with snow on the ground and hanging on branches. And blazing red leaves underneath. What a treat! Again, a once-in-a-lifetime treat. Who is there to thank for such an experience, but God? I am not arrogant or narcissistic enough to believe it was done for us. But the beauty of it makes me want to believe that.

Our trip coming back into the city was fraught with ambivalence. It felt like home, but we didn't welcome the noise and angry busyness of the traffic.

Why are people so angry? Perhaps there are too many people in one place which can't support them—not enough traffic markers, not enough policemen. We are always in a hurry. Hurrying frustrates everybody. No one has time for the niceties.

One gets the truth, but it always seems to be the angry truth. There is a defensive stance. I find myself getting into it, afraid I'll be violated, taken advantage of, used. So I defend myself in my space. "No" is easier to say here... but it is a sort of untruthful "no"—or at least a half-truthful "no"—an automatic "no," without thinking (much as "yes" is in southern culture and, so I have heard, in Asian cultures). My experience of Asians here is that they simply say nothing.

Today is a holiday. Columbus Day, I think. I took pleasure in seeing fewer people when I ran this morning. I'm getting to be like a resident New Yorker—delighting when the "tunnel and bridge" people, the commuters, stay at home. It was a quiet, sunny holiday.

We didn't go to church yesterday, and I didn't miss it. I wonder if I'd really miss it if I went only occasionally? Probably, but I'm not sure.

I must be out of the rhythm of doing business. I find the business of figuring out checks and dealing with money and bills to be a violent intrusion. I resent it terribly. The smallest little transaction I hate. This

Morning Run

angers me, but also confuses me. I experience confusion and depression over that. This can't last or I'll never make it at home. I do it now, but it takes longer.

TUESDAY

A nice, quiet day yesterday. And dinner last night with the Martins and the Fenhagens at the Martins' club (The Union League). What a place that was. Twenty-foot ceilings in panelled rooms, pure elegance. Right there at Park and Thirty-seventh Street. Outside was the traffic and the noise and the poor crazy folks and the filth. Inside was order, grace, beauty, opulence. The contrasts in this city are amazing and they are everywhere. The Columbus Day parade yesterday had Chinese teenagers dressed in kilts, playing bagpipes. What a hodgepodge, so typical of New York!

I am fifty-three years old today. God, that seems so old to me! I have always been haunted by death, the fear of it, the dread of non-being. I still think about it a lot. But it was always so very far off before. Now it is not so far—or at least not as far.

The cliches are really true. Day by day they are more true. "Make every day count." And "Think about what you do and value every day." I don't do that enough. Days just fade away, forgotten as a dream in the morning. I want to remember every day and every thing, but I don't.

I look so old. The cold air here has made my long gray hair so very straight. It looks straggly. No suntan leaves me pale. Wretched man that I am! Who will deliver me from this body of death?

I feel my life is fading, whimpering toward its end, not banging! What will be the next challenge? What to do next? I loved Jim Fenhagen's story of the priest who retired at 65, took an acting class, came up here, and now gets jobs as an actor. That's exciting.

Our dear friend, Helen, said one time, "When I die, I want to be used up, not left over." God, do I

October

agree! But, I'm scared I don't have the creativity I used to. I'm afraid I couldn't write a musical or a cantata or a book of prose or poetry as I use to imagine doing someday. I believe that muse has left me. I'm fearful I don't have the energy to do something like All Saints' again. I do All Saints' better (at least I believe I do that better) than I do anything else. But what could the anything else be?

Allison is not that excited now about what she does either. I wondered at the table last night, has she found her thing in life? I'm her thing. She is so very kind to me; her humor cheers my soul. It's amazing after all these years; we're still comfortable and fun together. Most of that reality depends on her. Life has been a free gift for me, full of grace. Allison is the greatest grace. Happy birthday! Indeed!

WEDNESDAY

My birthday gift from Atlanta friends Charlie and Harriet was a sumptuous meal with all the trimmings at the Quilted Giraffe. It's a swanky (very modern decor, stainless steel walls, aqua and pink, fixed menu), surprisingly small restaurant. We were treated like royalty. Charlie had called yesterday and ordered champagne and special wine. No telling what it cost! I've learned to receive gracefully, but not without some guilt.

The tension of celebrating and knowing some people are starving within blocks is a parable of my constant quandary: too much for me, too little for others. No pat answers work for me about this. Others seem to have an easier time with it than I.

Why won't I give up feeling guilty about my blessings, or do something about sharing them more than I do now? Guilt solves nothing unless it leads to action. The truth is I'm more grateful for the care and love that offers the celebration than the feast itself. That is how I am truly blessed, by the givers, not as much the gifts.

Morning Run

God has blessed me with so many givers and their generosity and graciousness always brings me to my knees! Thanks! Amen! Happy Birthday!

THURSDAY

Long wonderful day. However, working this morning, trying to pay bills and straighten out bank statements was very frustrating! I can't seem to get with that sort of thing any more. I seem confused and inept.

The play for our class yesterday was *Checkmates*—a fine, amazing quartet of actors that included Paul Winfield, Ruby Dee, Denzel Washington. The subject: two black couples, one young urban professional, one our age.

It points up to me that powerful, feeling performances can move even a mediocre script. Whereas sleepy, low-energy performances, e.g., *Broadway Bound* and *Speed the Plow*, in better-written scripts, don't move or impress me. The relationship is always there evidently: poor scripts can't even survive with good performances, but power-filled performances can inspire mediocre scripts. And poor performances can kill excellent scripts. The implications for sermons and preaching are undeniable!

After *Checkmates*, we went to the line at *Phantom of the Opera* and began to wait for cancellations and returns. At the beginning, we were number eleven and number twelve in the line. It was an amazing afternoon. It was almost instant community. We got to know very quickly a large variety of people from all over the country. It was actually fun. I kept saying as we sat there on the sidewalk in our bluejeans and running shoes, "If folks at All Saints' could see us now!"

And what a strange combination is this New York stew! The first person in line was a woman in her early forties. She had been waiting since morning, having not gotten in at the matinee. She was our expert, rightly in the number one slot. She was dressed in a blue denim miniskirt, black tights, tall cowboy boots with high heels, and a blue jean jacket covered with shiny studs. On the back was written, in rhinestones, "I love Las Vegas." She got the first ticket, of course, and it was a box seat. She was electrified with excitement and we all were thrilled with her; one of ours had succeeded! I thought she might light up like Robert Redford in *The Electric Horseman*. A well-dressed preppie woman in her thirties was next. She was a V.P. from L.A. with AT&T—the alphabet lady. She became friendly with a rotund guy, whom we discovered was attending the same convention as she, from Arkansas. I wonder if they'll ever see each other again. Both were single. He was number five.

A couple from Copenhagen was somewhere in there. They didn't speak English very well, but somehow managed to tell us about their grown children and the difficulties of their vacation time in America. He had a fetching twinkle in his eyes and she had one of those smiles you would swear was eternal. It was so bright!

Number six was a kid from New Hampshire down here for a computer school. He had a short mustache, a young bride back home, and was reading a book on dog training. He knew nothing about *Phantom* but figured he'd try to go where the crowd was.

Finally, we got in to see the show with our new friends on the last row of the balcony. What excitement! Our Las Vegas cowgirl leader stood and waved from her elegant box seat. We all cheered her and waved back triumphantly.

And... what a show! It is the best we've seen so far. It was moving. It was stunning.

Underneath (and almost in spite of) the glitz is a theme about encountering and facing the Dark—the allure of it and the fear of it, all at the same time. Somewhere between, but including revulsion and attraction,

Morning Run

is the dark and the ugly. But this is the creative energy—it instructs us, it calls forth creativity. It writes "the music of the night." It is Eros!

When, Christine (curiously, Christ) finally kisses the unmasked, ugly phantom, he loses his power over her. Beyond curiosity (she has removed his mask in act one) she kisses head-on this monster, and almost immediately he cuts down Raoul her lover and encourages her and her lover to leave, to escape—quickly, to move out—in effect, to be free!

It was a powerful moment when Christine kissed the unveiled, scarred face of the phantom. It touched me somewhere very deep. I almost gasped out loud. There was a collective, full silence. It was one of those theatrical moments that opens up experiences beyond the here and now. Something in the unconscious rises to the surface. Not clearly, but nevertheless there. The kid from New Hampshire who had waited in line with us wept out loud at that moment and Allison patted his arm. Something really happened! Perhaps one who has not acknowledged vulnerability would not be touched by that kiss, but most all were. We were shocked, or moved, or something. It was a pregnant silence. I shall never forget it. Even now, my eyes fill up as I remember.

And what magnificent liturgy: color, movement, music, drama, lighting, magic! What the church could learn from the theater! We in the church gave birth to the theater, and now we've lost our own offspring. The Protestant Reformation took to extremes the values of rationality and ethics. Put those two together and you get arid moralism. And so the theater left us.

For now, after the Enlightenment and the Reformation, it's the Phantom's "music of the night" that touches more folk than talking about sin in a conceptual way. The play speaks to the Dark, not in profound ways, but in popular ways that touch us all.

October

FRIDAY

Yesterday, Allison and I were on the subway heading to the Village for our class in American theater. It was a glorious fall day: clear and sunny and bright. Sitting side by side, we had been chattering on about nothing in particular, when a rather distinguished-looking black man leaned over and began to speak. I literally jumped. "Hope you'll forgive a spiritual observation," he said. I relaxed with the word spiritual; at least he wasn't threatening us! He continued, "You folks can't fool me!" (I tightened up again.) "I've been watching you since you got on the train, and I've decided you're really two eighteen-year-olds trying to look like you're fifty!" He showed an enormous, friendly grin. Then he was out the doors, moving down the platform, still smiling to himself, and disappearing in the crowd. We were startled mute, but we were smiling.

His observation was astute. That's how we've come to feel lately, all of eighteen again, exploring all the city (can this many people truly live together in one place?), devouring the arts (are they not all religious?), experiencing the church from the "outside" (what really is its purpose?), relishing our relationship (after 32 years, why do we have such a good time together?), reflecting on our souls (how are we doing in the third and final act?).

Also, like older teens, we're feeling curiosity about what we'll do and be when we grow up. We're anxious and exhilarated about new experiences and new possibilities. We're increasingly aware of the non-essential frills. We're more and more alarmed over rampant, cynical greed as the disparity between rich and poor gets greater. Most of all, we are experiencing a peculiar combination of arrogance and humility in a sort of second naivete as we are born again, perhaps not as children, but at least with eighteen-year-old eyes!

Surely our subway companion yesterday was an angel in disguise with a message of truth and grace!

Morning Run

Sometimes I wonder if one place can keep receiving people from all over the world and not lose its identity? Will "we" finally not be? I look at the Statue of Liberty on my morning run and I wonder and puzzle. Can she light the way for too many more? Will the rubberband holding us altogether in this hodgepodge nation finally snap? Or (and this is staggering to think of, but it enters my mind frequently), has it already snapped? How will Americans define themselves?

New York seems to be invaded by Asians: Chinese, Japanese, Vietnamese, and Korean. Everywhere. I must confess that they all look alike to me. It seems that they can't speak English, but they can certainly count money. They have taken over the deli market in New York.

Am I becoming anti-Asian? It's amazing how deep these prejudices must be in me. Perhaps they come from World War II, with the slant-eyed pilots in the picture shows who were the personification of evil, bombing Pearl Harbor and all that! It's interesting, however, that I've never seen an Asian person living on the streets, begging in the subway, or sleeping on the grates.

Ninety-nine-and-nine-tenths percent of street people and beggars I see are black. On the subway, at times, the whole car is black except me. Not at rush hour, but at other times. It is the great divide—the blacks underground on the trains and the whites above in the limousines and the buses. Cab drivers are generally white (not black or Asian), but they don't seem to speak English very well either. In fact, sometimes I've wondered if English is a secondary language in New York. On the subway, on the street, I hear every other language. I am the one who is a minority.

Language on the streets is amazingly vulgar, graphic, visceral. "Fuck" is the major verb and adjec-

October

tive I hear while I'm walking down the street. I overhear "fuck," "fucking," "fucker" all the time in snatches of conversation, in the crowds of button-downed, briefcase-carrying people scurrying around the Seaport at lunch and cocktail hour, on subway platforms, at tables next to ours in restaurants, waiting in line at the bank—everywhere! That's a real change from the streets of Atlanta at lunch time. "Shit" is a second runner-up word for use. And "Jesus" is a primary expletive as well! Except it's "Jee-suz!"

I'm not sure what this means, but it must have something unconsciously to do with basics: sex, excrement, and what? God? the Mystery? Fuck, Shit, Jesus. Why? Maybe in our chrome-veneered, outwardly shiny existence, there is a longing for the fleshiness, the earthiness, the messiness of the real world. And Jesus is that infleshed Mystery. I don't know, but there's something in that. I don't believe it's simply profanity. Why are these words so much more acceptable nowadays? I use them myself on occasion. It's not just coincidental; something significant is going on when suddenly language makes a quick dive for the gutter and takes Jesus with it!

SATURDAY

This morning is quiet, thank goodness. It's sunny and the paper/coffee/ juice, laidback, relaxed atmosphere is most welcome! Will I ever get "up" again to do and see as before? Sometimes that worries me.

Tonight we are to meet our good friends from Atlanta, the Davises, at the Plaza and then on to the Rainbow Room for supper. Tomorrow we screen a movie for our class, attend church at St. Bartholomew's, and see the Martha Graham Company at the theater. It sounds like too much—too exhausting to think about. Oh, and also one night next week is with Tom and Margaret, our old friends from way back. He

45

Morning Run

is now the rector of fashionable and powerful St. Bartholomew on Park Avenue.

That pace at home would be fairly normal for us. Dear God, I hope I can keep that up at home. But do I really want to? What does it mean that it both scares me and I dread it? I feel dread thinking about, anticipating, seeing all those people whom I basically like to be with. I dread dressing up in a tie. Ugh! What does all that mean? What do my feelings of dread mean?

SUNDAY

Dinner at the Rainbow Room was absolutely wonderful—not the dinner as much as the place itself and the magnificent view of the city at night. It was a relaxed time with Win and Tread, and I fundamentally enjoyed it and relished the company and the revolving dance floor and the art deco look of the renovation. I am so thankful for evenings like this which don't seem rushed and yet are full and fun and rewarding. I want more evenings like this at home.

MONDAY

Yesterday was a very crowded day, at least by our present standards. We were late for the nine o'clock service at St. Bart's. Margaret waves to us from the back of the church to join her. Half of the nave is separated by an enormous, transparent, gauze banner that hangs from the ceiling. It gives an illusion that the church is smaller than it really is.

There are hangings in the church everywhere, with felt cut-outs. Behind the altar there's one that says, "St. Bart's Nine O'Clock am Service." The book handed us by the ushers is called "St. Bart's Book." Actually, it is excerpts from the Prayer Book for the liturgy and some psalms and hymns. Included were my songs, "Surprise" and "Celebrate," but without my name as the author.

October

There was guitar accompaniment to the singing and no organ music. Tom's sermon was rambling and long, though lively (as he always is). In today's church that covers a multitude of sins!

Margaret is exuberant, a smile that ignites, and just fundamentally jolly! I like her! I like them both! We are invited there next week for supper and I look forward to spending some time with them. They are very interesting and animated people. We all want to talk at the same time. Allison says on occasions in the past we have gotten so excited that no one listens. On that evening, I hope we don't do that.

Occasionally, there is a certain sadness about Tom, and maybe Margaret as well. He has fought long and hard over building a tower on the corner at St. Bart's. Maybe somehow their struggle here tends to make more hallowed the wind and fire at St. Luke's, Atlanta, years ago. And they can't, nor should they, let go of that powerful renewal. I understand that from my St. Thomas experience in Huntsville in the sixties where the freedom and joy of new liturgy and commitment set the place ablaze. Yet today in St. Bart's there were probably a couple of hundred folks at the nine o'clock service. That's sad. Also, the passing of the peace seemed forced to me. I don't know, it all had a hollow ring. The service seemed very parochial. Maybe all parishes in New York are parochial. Maybe all parishes in general are parochial. I am certainly parochial about All Saints'. Who knows? Maybe it was only *me*. But it just all seemed somewhat forced, like cocktail party intimacy. Perhaps I yearn for something that does not exist anymore... gone with the wind... at least for me.

After church, we were off for the screening of *1969* at Lowe's Astor Theater on Times Square. It was a moving film up to a point. Allison and I both cried. Vietnam, hippies, peace and flowers, our own lost dreams of a new order shattered by assassins' bullets. And here

Morning Run

we are now with yuppie greed, conservative fear, and more dope and crime and poverty and waste and decadence. God, it seems so depressing sometimes against the backdrop of the exuberance of 1969 and the Age of Aquarius.

Like the sixties, the movie also fell to pieces at the end. It got schmaltzy and sentimental. It really got so bad that I quit crying in the middle of a good cry! I resented the unfulfilled promises of the movie, as I resent the unfulfilled promises of the sixties. No doubt my experience of St. Bart's is filtered this morning through the raw memories of *1969*.

Later we had a nice brunch at Un, Deux, Trois, a small French restaurant on Forty-fourth Street. We walked up to the City Center Theatre, very sleepy and tired, for the Martha Graham concert.

Well, bang! Bang! What a marvelous surprise! The Martha Graham Company was vigorous and graceful and real and visceral and athletic. We sat so close (on the second row) we could hear the dancers breathing and see the sweat and hear the grunts. It was breathtaking, moving beyond words: heavy and light, tragic and comic.

It was magnificent liturgy, liturgy in the ancient and grand tradition of rites and rituals around fires and primitive worship. Maybe liturgy in the ancient tradition is not so "primitive." Maybe ours has gotten too civilized, too nice, too cerebral. Classical ballet is like what some professional liturgists call "good" liturgy. I find it stilted, only hinting at the depths of true liturgy. Classical ballet, to me, is effete, cerebral, prissy, like so-called good liturgy.

But this stuff! God, it's what true liturgy is really about: controlled, barely controlled, chaos. It was natural, but very disciplined. Every movement (hands, heads, feet, eyes), all of it was intentional, off-center but satisfying—a glimpse into anti-structure. On the line, on the threshold of structure.

October

And what beauty. Sheer physical beauty. I wished they were dancing absolutely nude. Yet, Graham uses the costumes in her choreography. It is not just the natural (bodies) but also human created stuff (the material and fabric of dresses and tights). All are part of the moving sculpture. Just as liturgy should be. It was, indeed, a religious experience.

We had a long wait on the subway platform at Columbus Circle, due to some problem with the track. For the first time, I helped a poor black man, almost naked, who was begging for help and for food. I bought a hot dog and a grape drink at the stand and took them to him, where he was lying down, holding his stomach, crying out and writhing in pain. No one, including us, even looked at him. He looked up and thanked me. I felt hollow and inadequate.

WEDNESDAY

We went to the Cloisters of the Metropolitan Museum of Art yesterday in our class, and it was absolutely beautiful. The setting on the Hudson and the gorgeous view of autumn colors lining the water made me aware of how, in the city, I miss the trees and open spaces.

The museum was naturally quiet on my soul. Medieval architecture everywhere, of course. The chants over the speaker and the serenity of the place were a needed break from city energy and movement. It's a different kind of energy: the empowerment of quietness, a link with the past, the ongoingness of the tradition. The comfort, the solace of the old and the elegant. All of this bestows a sort of renewing quiet in me. Yes, that's it. Quiet—not the absence of sound, not the absence of anything—but being filled up with quiet, not only in sound but in sights and shapes that are simple and solid and uncluttered.

Late-Medieval gothic gets noisy. It's fussy. Stained glass windows, painted arches, painted statues,

Morning Run

gold chalices are not so quietly filling. Medieval Gothic gets noisy like a modern city. There must be something for our times—for "retreating" in the urban context—with the idea of being filled with quiet. Symbolically at least. It is not the absence of all noise, but the filling up with simple quiet. Not retreating exactly, but pursuing intentionally this arena; this setting, the fullness of quiet.

Dinner with Ben from Atlanta last night at the Bridge Cafe was relaxing and comfortable. We had to cancel engagements with two other couples from home. I need to cancel more at home. I need to think about that more later. But it's off to the Met now and to the Degas exhibit.

THURSDAY

Wednesday morning was Degas. What an experience! I was so glad for the individual earphones with tapes. It gave me the illusion that I was alone. I would not have wanted Lucia and Pete (parents of All Sainters who generously got us the tickets) or anybody at all to intrude on my experience. Even Allison would have been an intrusion, as it turned out, because I got so caught up in myself. We all experienced the exhibit alone in a great crowd of people.

The Degas exhibit is enormous and covers his first to his last work. I was overcome with the intensity of his figures—so alive, so dramatic, so human and ethereal—a sort of incarnated luminous quality in them.

"The Bathers," painted toward the end of his life—with the gaping, empty tubs (sarcophagi?)—was very, very moving. I stood in the middle of the gallery, surrounded by a crowd of people, and wept. The red and orange of the woman arranging her hair did me in. In her look was beauty, ecstasy, pain, and even terror and violence. Its reds almost burned me up. It was a moment.

The next room with the last painting—the jockey fallen off his horse, dead, with no right hand—stopped

October

me still. I thought I would cry out loud. I heard on the tape that Degas had been completely blind for the last twenty years of his life. I could not believe it! I thought of Beethoven's being deaf toward his life's end.

Then I saw Allison across the gallery. I wished no one was here but the two of us. I would have collapsed in her arms in tears. But no. I am in control, with all these people in a public place.

Our class on drama afterwards was okay, but I simply was spent. I could not even listen to the lecture very well.

The Degas experience left me with one overpowering insight. He got better, freer, more creative with color and form and line and subject, as he got older! His earlier work was technically, naturally, realistically better, but it did not have the power or the sweeping movement of his later work. He got better all through his life. God, help me to do that. Please. I may need to change my medium as he did. But don't ever let me quit trying new things and new contexts and new ways to paint. Please. I am touched and excited and empowered by this possibility. Thanks be to God.

FRIDAY

Last night we had supper with Jerry, an old priest friend from Oklahoma. Somehow his life is a sad commentary on him and the church. He does everything. He attends every conference. He's been to Israel to study. He's gotten some advanced degree from Harvard. He's always a delegate at General Convention. He leads this or that board. He's taken a special trip to Australia because he's on the board of some ecumenical organization. He's headed to Africa with a Methodist interchange. But he is so out of touch! He does not understand! He somehow can't connect! He is so goodhearted and he tries, but he just cannot connect himself and the real church and the real world. His church,

Morning Run

his world and mine are not the same church or even the same world. It's very sad to me. Allison says he'll probably be a bishop someday. But he's too old, I think. Maybe she is right. I think he is so terribly sad. It just never worked out for him the way he wanted it to, I bet.

And as for me? I don't know how it (whatever it is) will work out either!

SATURDAY

The movie *Mystic Pizza* yesterday was an absolute delight. It was so warm and gentle and lovely; I hated for it to be over. It was a wet and rainy and stormy day. Messing around in the rain (stepping in puddles, having wet feet) brings realism to any romantic notion about the streets of New York.

There are always beggars there in the streets, in the subways, jingling their paper cups with change. Their incessant, unceasing jingling crowds me no end. I feel peculiarly angry and sad. I'm guilty for not helping, and yet irritated, doubting that they are in dire trouble. Surely, there are other things for them to do. Surely . . . we need to make other things to do.

The grate people really get to me on a cold day like today—all huddled under paper and old blankets on top of the grates where warm air comes up against the side of building. There are several down the street on Gold Street, near the park. The sun shines there in the morning, and there are crowds of people. But there they also sleep, not moving. I wonder sometimes if they're dead! Yet, they're there every morning. Perhaps they are dead. I wonder what in the world they did on a stormy night like last night.

The subways are a disconcerting experience. I've gotten so accustomed to all the beggars there, I hardly think of it anymore.

All sorts and conditions of people for sure! No one talks. No one looks at anyone else. Many people read

October

on the subway or sleep. In the rush of people stacked beside other people, body against body, alone, you can hear breathing, but no eye contact and no words. It's as though we pretend we are alone but the pretense does not work, because we fear the intimacy of eye contact. Body contact is a necessity; we're so crowded. But not our eyes! Car after car after car of bodies. Stacked in the cars, like Jews going to the death camps, the subway death camp express!

I've started watching everybody. What faces! All sorts and every sort. Can God really care about each one? What a romantic, childish, even narcissistic and arrogant idea! Every one of them—the whole car full of silent, vacant-eyed people—are his? It is too quaint.

But that's what we affirm. The old folk song sings, "All are precious in his sight, Jesus loves the little children of the world!" Yesterday, a very beautiful young woman with long blond hair and very fair skin and a lovely gentle face came on the train with her baby boy in a stroller. He was sucking a bottle and holding it himself in one hand. He had a blue New York baseball cap pulled down over his head and tiny little tennis shoes on his feet.

I was looking down. He turned his head and began to flirt. I looked behind me to see who was the object of his playful flirtation. It was a middle-aged black woman, nicely dressed, playing with him by wagging her head. Another person seated across the car was smiling too. And then another, and another. The mother was vacant-faced, never acknowledging anything, dead for all I knew. But soon I noticed several people on our end of the car come alive. No longer were they blank faces with no eyes. A scary-looking black boy lost his cool and was smiling. He tapped out the rap rhythm from his earphones on his knees for the baby to see.

That is the ultimate defense on the subway, against the dangers of attack and rape and robbery and

Morning Run

murder, or anonymity or fierce loneliness, or cynicism or death. A baby—the smiling, unassuming, unprotected face of a baby. Perhaps naively, I think: no one could do harm in the presence of that face. Surely... surely... "and a little child shall lead them."

SUNDAY

I'm feeling overwhelmed with things to do, too many people to see, the same old patterns for me. Allison seems to like seeing people still, but I'm fed up with it—I feel crowded. We won't have any time, I begin to think. I won't have *my* time. The old feelings at home of having no time for myself are beginning to come back. But in reality there is not really that much to do. It feels like too much, but it is not too much.

Last night with Mary and Frank was nice, good food—and it was like home. They were passing through New York on the way back to Atlanta after a cruise. I only hope we can have their vitality and good cheer when we're eighty! Allison and I rode home on the bus at midnight, tired and full.

I don't know why I'm feeling so crowded today, when it's a bright, sunny Sunday morning. Could Sunday have something to do with my feelings? I've just spent an hour or so reading and loving the *New York Times*. And I begin to think that I'm not so sure that I can subscribe to it in Atlanta. It would be depressing without the possibility of doing and going and experiencing what is written about there.

I am dreading going home to Atlanta today to the same old things. It makes me think about the future. What do I want to accomplish still? How do I want to be remembered? It seems so futile to think about. Also, I'm tired of being passed over for bishop. I hate being passed over. Always. It's not so much that I want to be a bishop or that I covet the job. But I don't like being passed over when I decide to be in the running.

October

Also I am sad and angry at the political scene. Bush seems so silly. Quayle seems to be the quintessential yuppie of the 80s—pretty, dumb, and greedy. Something gets to me about all of that. I think of myself as someone who doesn't pick the winner. But I voted for Kennedy—and for Carter—and for Fowler—and for Young. So my feelings are not supported totally by the facts.

And likewise I don't think of myself as being a winner. But again, I was elected president of my junior high fraternity, and was president of Jasons in college, and president of my class in seminary, and I was vice-president many times. Yet, most often I have been the non-winner leader. I've not felt recognition by the masses. I'm more appointable than electable. I'm more chosen than raised up. God, I'm working myself into really being agitated this morning. I do want challenge, but I don't want to be overcrowded with too much to do.

Please, hang with me, God. I am narcissistic and whiny today. I feel forgotten, even though I know that is terribly neurotic. Maybe I *want* to feel that way this Sunday morning. Good Lord deliver me.

Later today, we're going to *Anything Goes* and then attending a fancy dinner at General Seminary. Also to church at St. James at 11:15. Perhaps that will cheer me up. But somehow today, I don't want to be cheered up. I want to wallow, wallow, wallow in my feelings of non-recognition and the triumph of fools, and the power of greed, and the stupidity of most people (but certainly not me!) and the injustice of everything. It's not sadness I feel but anger, I guess. I am an angry person. Good Lord, deliver me again.

I think these kinds of feelings started with Papa. I need to get my Papa off my back! He is dead and gone. But not with me. I am still angry at him for not recognizing me, for others not realizing the truth about him in relationship to me. How he withheld approval

Morning Run

and affection. He was forever critical of me, forever deprecating. Not one single time did he ever tell me that I did well or that he cared about me. Not once! It was as though he feared giving affirmation to anything I achieved except perfection; 95 on an exam meant I missed 5; vice-president meant I was a failure.

All of these musings are both not true and very true at the same time. I'm not talking rationally, but about how I *felt* growing up and can so easily feel again. In a strange way, I really loved him and wanted desperately to please him. I realize he had no father model, and Mama assures me that he did love me. Everybody says that he was a good man. I don't doubt that. Yet there are two truths, two realities—mine and theirs. Theirs was a picture of an ethical, community-involved, generous, honest, and fun-loving citizen. Mine was a tyrannical, all-powerful, demanding, non-appreciating, and no-nonsense king! How confusing it was to believe my truth. As a child, I thought I was the one that was crazy. How could my perceptions of him be true in the face of what all the "big people" said? But those kinds of truths are self-evident. What everybody else feels doesn't matter to an eight year old! Sometimes I wonder if I would have ever survived without the unyielding, unswerving grace of Mama. Thank God for her.

In *Into the Woods* the Baker sings about fathers: "they disappoint, they disappear, they die, but they don't . . . no more curses you can't undo, left by fathers you never knew, no more questions . . . no more!" How my own Papa must have lived under that curse of a father he never knew! Poor little thing. And how I, also, live under the same curse!

And now, God, my papa and my mama, please deliver me from the curse of anger, from the confusion of two truths. Love me. Let me bathe in your grace, challenged and accepted and affirmed as before. Please. Please. Amen.

October

LATE SUNDAY

Tonight at the seminary was warm and gentle and old. The refectory is ancient and elegant, rich in tradition. It was lit with candlelight. It could have been a set for a movie. And it was lovely. It connects me with something other than the here and now.

Anything Goes was lilting and lifting! Brassy and funny. A clean script without too many frills. Old time Broadway Cole Porter. And the Vivian Beaumont Theater at Lincoln Center is attractive and unusual for a musical. Almost in the round.

All in all this evening soothed gently my ruffled soul with the oil of gladness. Thanks.

MONDAY

Yesterday we decided to attend church at St. James on Madison Avenue. It was a pretty day so we got the car out, having an easy drive up the FDR and over to Madison. I even got a parking place directly across the street. Since this was an uptown church, we dressed rather nicely—Allison in her Sunday clothes and me in a suit and tie. We hurried up the front steps and were greeted by a female usher. I found this a little unusual since I expected conservative St. James at 11:00 to be almost morning coats and men only. When I glanced at my program, it seemed to be Morning Prayer and no communion. So I asked the usher, "Will there be no communion?" She said, "No, we had that at 9:00." I said, "Well, thanks very much, but we're going to find us a eucharist." And we pleasantly turned around and went back to the car with Allison grumbling something to the effect that if she was going to get dressed up and come to church, she certainly expected the full course!

Now we were faced with the problem of where to go at 11:05 for a eucharist. Perhaps we could get to the Cathedral in time.

Morning Run

We raced madly up the east side, turning at the top of the park up into Harlem. I'm aware that Allison is so fascinated with the scenery that she seems not to notice my fast driving. On to Riverside Drive past a literal war zone of burned out territories, we finally discovered the Cathedral, after first confusing it with Riverside Church.

Again, miracle of miracles, we found a parking place out front (not a totally legitimate one) and rushed into the dark and musty cavernous structure.

When my eyes adjusted to the dimness, I knew I was home. We passed by all sorts of displays, hurrying to our seats, guided by another female usher. The sermon was being preached by an unvested person whom I could not understand. I discovered from the program that he is the President of the United Nations; it is U.N. Sunday. I didn't listen very well because I was too busy looking around at the sights and the people. There were people from everywhere: black, white, yellow, young, old, rich, poor, American, foreign. Tourists moved around the side seeming not to notice the Holy Mysteries taking place at the enormous altar, which is down in the transept and not up where the high altar was originally designed to be.

At the announcement time, the Dean described all sorts of activities and services: a special meeting with Jesse Jackson on issues of the homeless beginning at one o'clock, a concert with stars from the theater to raise money for AIDS ministries, a special reading of poetry by the Cathedral poet-in-residence, and a veritable three ring circus of offerings. I whispered to Allison, "This is what a cathedral or any large urban parish ought to be!" She smiled and squeezed my hand.

To receive the communion we gathered in a large circle around the altar. The acolyte showing us to our place turned out to be a young Spanish friend of ours from All Saints', a restoration architect who had moved

October

to New York. We all embraced with happy words, exchanged phone numbers, and made promises to meet before we go home. How amazingly small the Episcopal Church really is!

All in all, yesterday was a fascinating pilgrimage: nice, flat, ordered morning prayer at St. James, the war-torn desert of Harlem, and the carnival of color and celebration of St. John the Divine. It really was divine! The divine march continues. But who's the drum major and where's it headed? Somehow our Cathedral experience gives me hope that at least we're in the right parade!

WEDNESDAY

The Barber of Seville yesterday was long and boring. Some of the music was familiar, and it was spectacularly done. Yet Kathleen Battle was very weak. Her voice was not that clear and certainly not powerful. Perhaps she was holding back, since it was a dress rehearsal.

The Met building was very fifties, but nice. It was a pretty day and we ate a picnic snack that we took with us, seated on the red carpet ramp inside the building. There were many school children there for the rehearsal and other picnickers for the performance at eleven a.m. We were not out until after two o'clock.

As we were leaving to go to class this morning, I could not find my watch (I found it kicked under the table when we returned). Somehow that just threw me. I felt inept and old. I felt dumb. I hate to feel dumb.

Maybe I've been out of role too long. But why do I feel that now? I have not contributed anything to anybody in a very long while. Maybe that's it. But none of those observations rings completely true.

I just can't write any more today. Nothing will come out. I'm longing to say something profound, but I'm not able to. I'm just wanting to vegetate, be a

Morning Run

couch potato. I'm depressed, with no energy. I must get over this and through this, and I will.

Perhaps we have done too much and had too much stimulation. Too many theaters. I don't get moved quickly any more. It's all so ho hum. We've seen so much. Maybe I need a retreat from stimulation.

And I will get through this, I'm sure. My old friend and bishop, Bill, is coming for dinner tonight and I have a class at the Met today. I'll read some at the seminary too. My reading there makes me feel like I have accomplished something. I don't know why I need to feel like I have accomplished something.

Nouwen talks in *Life Signs* about the necessary dimension of fecundity in our spiritual lives; he distinguishes between producing something and being fruitful, which to me means letting new things come to birth. I do really need to do that. And in that sense, I need to accomplish something, to give birth—fecundity.

I suddenly remember a fragment of a dream I had last night. I have a baby. I actually deliver a baby boy! Allison is there holding my hand. That's all I remember. I look away from my writing, thinking of the dream, trying to recall more, when suddenly I hear (no, not really audibly) but I hear nevertheless (not with my ears), "I am your midwife." There is no one there in my open eyes. All I see is the flicker of morning sun across the blinds. And I say out loud, "Good Lord, but what is the new baby's name?"

THURSDAY

I feel much better this morning; although I didn't sleep much without heat! The nuns must be out of town; and they forgot to turn on the heat, which is regulated from their apartment. I finally get up about 5:45 am and took an early run in the dark. It was beautiful. I watched the moon over the Hudson River and the rippling of the sparkles on the water. In the dark, the Statue of

October

Liberty shown like a beacon. Battery Park City and New Wintergarden were stunning all lit up.

My class at the Met yesterday was on Renaissance art, completely religious in symbols and expression, mostly from Christ's life. We moved from more Byzantine, stylized works to opulent, rounded, realistic, as in Raphael. The colors were very rich.

The church was the depository of the arts! Theology was never separate from anything in those days. It was assumed that arts were expressions of faith. Certainly they were in Medieval times and into the Renaissance. Why did the split between faith and art take place? When did the split take place? Can the church reclaim that place? That relationship? I would guess not. It really is over, this marriage of theology and art. But it doesn't need to be a messy, hostile divorce.

How can we get along better and use the arts for religious expression and evangelism? How can we use the arts to bridge the gap between this world and the Mystery? As an integral part of spiritual life? As a way to be centered and focused and grounded?

How can the arts help us to be more integrated and less fragmented, less hurried and more whole? How can the arts be natural, an assumed part of life—not tangential, or tacked on for the upper class? Can art not just be adorning but essential to life in the city? I think it must become that.

Quality becomes critical then—whatever quality is. How is it determined? Good movies, good plays, good paintings—what makes them *good*? Is it their ability to point toward the Mystery? To point beyond themselves? To what degree are they icons, and not idols? To the degree that they point to God? Is that a valid criterion for good or valuable art? Is this an operative value, the ability of the work to transcend itself? Move me out of myself, toward God? Toward the good, toward the beautiful?

Morning Run

What is a faithful aesthetic for Christians? Are good and beautiful the same? My hunch is they're pretty close. The beautiful might not be so good, but the good must also be beautiful. I think that it was Keats in "Ode on a Grecian Urn" who said, "Truth is beauty and beauty... truth. That is all ye know on earth and all ye need to know."

It's complex and abstract. How can such musings affect the average person in the pew? For me, another component of all of this is justice. Perhaps there are three realities in the dialectic or (should I say) trialectic when thinking about what is good: beauty (that which moves me), truth (that which is honest), and *justice* (that which gives value to things).

Beauty, truth, justice. Keats was too Greek, with truth and beauty alone. What keeps it Biblical, and I must say rings true to me, is to add the dimension of justice to an aesthetic. That means that what is *right* is also truthful and beautiful.

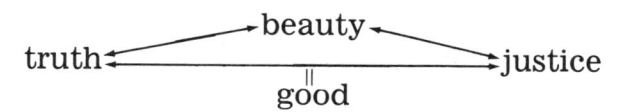

$$\text{truth} \leftrightarrow \overset{\text{beauty}}{\underset{\overset{\parallel}{\text{good}}}{}} \leftrightarrow \text{justice}$$

This seems like word games, but it's more than that. I need to struggle with this later.

FRIDAY

Shaw's *The Devil's Disciple* was excellent: wonderfully written, superbly acted. The Circle in the Square Theater is an interesting theater design for Broadway, put to good use with this play.

Shaw was pro-woman and anti-war and anti-clerical and anti-church; he seemed to see the power of grace as opposed to the power of the law. The play was filled through and through with Biblical references and allusions. But the audience missed all of them. At least almost all of them. One comic line assumed that the

October

audience would know that Paul studied with Gamaliel. But no one knew that, so no one laughed, but me.

It is truly a secular audience as opposed to Shaw's time, an audience that is biblically illiterate! Can a society with its Judeo-Christian roots exist without knowing the story? If we don't know any more where we come from, will the whole enterprise simply disintegrate?

Living in New York has made me suspect that American society might be over. The Visigoths, the Barbarians, have invaded the decadent Roman Empire and the whole thing is in disarray, what with drugs and crime and homelessness and the cynical politics of Reaganism, and shallow thought processes and sentimentality and complete rootlessness. The shallow conservatism so in vogue today is a curse we have brought on ourselves as a nation.

But... anyway... surely it will work out in the long run. But right now, I'm afraid the American experiment is simply not working. We cannot take in any more people. We have no common values, no community, and no ethics. The fabric of the country is tearing in two. And this city is the warning sign of what is to come. Is it, as Tom Wolfe says, the "bonfire of the vanities"? How despairing that sounds!

I feel pretty good today. The sun is shining and it's clear and it's cool. So these thoughts are not my psyche blackening everything I see. Living here in the filthy despair and the homelessness of the city, I lose hope about an easy future for our country.

On a late afternoon walk yesterday, I passed the porno shop (billed as an "adult bookstore") on Ann Street near Broadway, and decided to go in. Ah, the freedom of anonymity. I can go anywhere, anytime, and no one knows me. This place was an amazing cafeteria of lust. On the left, as I walked in, were shelf after shelf of

Morning Run

magazines depicting on their covers every possible form of conjugal union—male/female—male/male—female/female. On the covers no less! I picked up one and found they were all sealed in plastic. One must pay to look past the cover.

My first thought, peculiarly, was that all these models were, at one time, little girls and little boys. They must have been the joy of their mamas and daddies, surely for a little while. What happened along the way? Do we all just grow up, or do we grow down? It is sure that we lose our puppy innocence, as well as our puppy looks!

To the rear of the place was a man exchanging money for tokens (like at the subway). Beyond him was a gallery of little closet-rooms where, if the token was deposited, pornographic movies, or at least portions of movies, appeared on a television screen. I exited that room rather quickly, feeling like I couldn't breathe.

On the other side, I was surprised to see above the entrance to another section of the place, a garish green and red neon sign that read, "The Jimmy Swaggart Room." I was curious enough to read the smaller sign by the door which said that at certain times (five to midnight, I believe) live models appeared there. For five dollars, one could watch the show. I did not go in.

There were steps to the right down into the basement. It was dark. Over the door was a sign that read, "The Bull's Pen." Because of the pictures on the wall, I deduced this was homosexual pornography. I decided not to go down the steps into the dark.

I left the yellow-lighted, yellow-painted establishment with ambiguous feelings of sadness and disgust and fascination and lust. As I walked down Fulton Street, I found myself singing the words from Shakespeare's sonnet, "What a piece of work is man, how noble in reason, how infinite in faculties." Are we, as the Psalmist says " . . . created a little lower than the angels?" Only a little lower?

October

MONDAY

I didn't write over the weekend in Boston. I was lazy and out of the routine. Boston was lovely and clean and slower-paced than New York. It was almost like a small town. I saw only a couple of street people. Even the lower socio-economic neighborhoods seemed well-groomed and cared for. Compared to New York, it was purity! People were more accommodating—a cab driver even started up a conversation with me. But service was less efficient than New York.

Yet in some mysterious way, a demon was over us. The bed-and-breakfast we had reserved turned out to be a first floor, crowded, tacky place. I stormed out into the street to get us another place to stay, leaving Allison behind. I finally found a room at the Marriott. I registered there; then took the key back to the bed-and-breakfast woman at her headquarters. She acted surprised. I was honest and firm, but not insulting. I lost my deposit, but not my temper, and I cancelled the rest of our time there and tore up the credit card receipt.

The tour guide on Saturday morning was simply awful. We did get around the city. but most of his stories were boring and he was busy telling personal anecdotes instead of pointing out the sights. It was a disaster. We left the tour and got a cab at the Old Ironsides Museum. Allison called the Grey Line office and complained after we got back to the motel. She decided to "take to her bed" in the Marriott all afternoon. I got a very good massage finally, but on the way to the gym the subway broke down and the shuttle bus was late. What a day of screw-ups!

Later we had dinner at a little French restaurant that wasn't bad. On Friday night, we ate a fair meal at a restaurant in an old house near the Colonnade Hotel. Quincy Market, located right across from the hotel, was absolutely wonderful. I hope that Underground Atlanta

Morning Run

can be as populated and as vital. I was glad that we walked to the Old North Church and Paul Revere's House on Sunday morning. In a way it redeemed the sightseeing part of the trip.

I had bad stomach cramps yesterday. Perhaps I was frustrated at how things were not working out. It amazes and disturbs me that I really hate people's inefficiency. It bothers me no end. It is my downfall. I react internally sometimes with horrible anger and even rage, disproportionate to the situation. I don't understand my own actions—why anger takes me over on such occasions. It's a demon! It's an unspecified angst. I've still got a little of it today.

Perhaps from dreams or the afterburn of the weekend, I woke up this morning in my rejection mode—the "I've never been appreciated" mode. It is so neurotic. When I feel this way, I rehearse all the occasions in my life when I feel I have not been appreciated or loved or valued. Why do I get so hooked? So taken with my own demon. Mostly, it's not true. This demon is an illusion—a big story that I've told myself. But it possesses me and it takes away the fullness of my life and destroys community. It's this demon that causes my cramps and my rage and my despair.

My rejection mode has enough truth in it, however, to trick me. To seduce me. It is not all truth, but it has a little bit in it. It is not *the* truth. I am pretty much loved and appreciated.

Sometimes I think it is a major miracle—a big grace—that I was chosen rector of All Saints'. It's the one and only time I ever really won anything significant. I'm always expected to win. I'm always thought of as one who wins. But the truth is, I am not a winner. I never have been very appreciated that way. But I am truly appreciated. I am truly loved, particularly in my "beloved community" at All Saints'. And it is not just by God, but by the community. I must remember that fundamental truth over and over and over and over.

NOVEMBER

November

TUESDAY

Yesterday was lovely. Thanks! Sunny and clear, a good chill in the air. I went to the library at General Seminary, had lunch at a deli next to the Seminary, then back to the library for lots of reading. All alone. That was so renewing—to be alone and not be lonely. I was pleasingly alone and enjoying my aloneness. Enjoying myself.

Then back home to a good supper of casseroles. God, how I've missed regular cooking. It's been so long, I've forgotten. We rode the subway to wait in line for *Phantom* tickets, and we were the last *not* to get tickets. I let a couple of single tickets go by, as well as some black market $100 tickets. So we took the subway back to 14th Street and the Halloween Parade.

It was glorious. Cold, but not windy. Crazy, but not sick. All sorts of folks—thousands in the parade and 250,000 watching. It was impossible to tell the marchers from the watchers, since they moved back and forth across the line. A really good spirit at the parade! Fun. The crowd was friendly.

People love to mask up and disguise themselves. What is it that makes another reality so enticing? The good spirit of the parade almost inferred that people mask and dress up and "come out," not as New York cool, aloof, or angry, but as warm genuine people. How strange ... to come out as warm people. Perhaps a disguise allows the real human person to come out in front, so to speak, of the costume. Just perhaps, for the moment, the blasé and defensive masks. which seem necessary to wear for protection in ordinary life, are lowered in the exuberance of the roleless parade. What a paradox! People put on masks in order to unmask. But how exhilarating and full of spirits—holy and evil!

Morning Run

Coming home, we had a near disaster in the subway station. We got off at a different stair and proceeded up and found ourselves locked in a section of bars. It was a tall turnstile that you could go in but you could not get back out of. A young man—handsome and slick and angry—was locked in with us. When we heard the next train come, we banged on the bars and yelled. Several people finally came and we sent them to get the guard who arrived and let us out.

It was a potentially dangerous experience. But neither I nor Allison was scared. When we thought about it later, we were panicked by what might have happened, locked in alone with a rapist, or locked in underground overnight, cold and freezing. Perhaps it was a footnote of warning for the evening: Don't be fooled by spirits—some of them are demonic and potentially dangerous. Discernment is necessary in the All Hallow's Eve Parade!

LATER TUESDAY

The election outcome seems fairly predictable, if the polls are right. I am still not sure why it upsets me so that nobody I ever vote for wins. It punches all my buttons, my insecurity about not winning. And of always being out of step. My out-of-step-ness is not altruistic, however. I like Fenhagen's parable in *Invitation to Holiness* about dancing to different music. But my dancing is not so pure. It doesn't feel like I'm different for any higher cause, such as the Gospel. It's a narcissistic aberration that I want people to notice me and recognize my idiosyncrasies as wonderful and lovable! All of that is selfish, and I must let it go.

I keep doing that with the political election—letting go, not worrying about it, trying to tell myself that it doesn't matter. But the election feels like a triumph of greed. It feels like the have-nots will get less, that nobody believes the poor are worse off under the

November

Republicans! Or that crime is up and dope is up because hopelessness and cynicism and militarism in federal budgets are up!

I really am afraid a breakdown in the system eventually will be necessary. And that may happen; the prophets would call it the judgment of God on an unjust, compassionless society. I certainly don't *want* it. I enjoy my creature comforts from being a "have." But I am willing to pay much more tax to solve the situations of homelessness and crime, and certainly drugs!

In some ways I fear going home to Atlanta! My colleagues might not allow me to change. I could be pushed into old roles. I need to define more precisely and clearly what I want to do and how I want to be different. Then they may have better ways to respond to what I want. Of course, I'll not know the ways I've changed unconsciously until I experience being home and others' reactions to me. It all seems complicated. Please help, Good Lord.

WEDNESDAY

Yesterday was glorious, in spite of the weather! It was cold and windy and very rainy. We splashed to the Met for a class—"The Baroque Period." We took a bus from there for a delicious lunch at a Japanese restaurant. We did not finish until about three o'clock. Then we saw *Another Woman*, Woody Allen's serious movie about trying to come to terms with being fifty, about doors that are closed and things that simply can't be undone. I do know about that. It was fine acting, but less than completely satisfying in its character development and emotional involvement. It was too cerebral.

Then we went home and dressed and took a taxi to Carnegie Hall for Bernstein's birthday concert. It was thrilling (we were way up on the fourth balcony) and what drama! It was a sold-out house, wonderful acoustics. Carnegie Hall has been beautifully renovated; it's

Morning Run

simple and understated, not opulent nor as rococo as Broadway theaters. The music was superlative. Bernstein is a real showman. He conducted the third movement of Brahms' Fourth Symphony with his head and his shoulders and his legs and his body, but not his hands or arms. I don't know why, but it was entertaining and apparently effective.

The phone is ringing all the time recently—people coming in and out of New York, wanting to see us. I feel so crowded, even by people that I like. So many people consider Allison and me available. I want to be considered available, but I don't want to be that available. I'm amazed that the recluse part of me is so big nowadays. Allison is much more interested in living her life with others lately. I'm much more into being alone. She tolerates being alone. I cherish it.

I'm not sure how this will be at home. I'm going to need to set some new parameters. I have to make do with new goals and expectations and payoffs for not always being available. I want to choose more carefully who and when and how I relate to others.

I'm afraid breaking out of old patterns may be too difficult in Atlanta. I may not be able to do it. I've read all the research on clergy sabbaticals, how the majority move within a year of returning. I may need to move. But if I move, I'll need to be very, very aware of my need for acceptance, which causes me to say yes and be available to everybody. For now I'm fairly secure in my role at All Saints', but I don't completely like the shape that role has taken. Sometimes I wonder, dear God, will I ever settle in—settle in anywhere? Probably not. When the time comes, help me to move for the right reasons and not just the neurotic ones.

THURSDAY

There's so much going on that I have to pause and ask myself, "Now, what did I do yesterday?" First, I ran—

November

cold, windy run. Then very casual, slow time, taking care of some letters and bills. I finally wrote the Rotary Club telling them they would have to expel me (rather than I readily resigning like a good southern gentleman) for missing too many meetings while I am on Sabbatical. It was a lazy morning—I love lazy mornings—piddling around, taking care of small tasks. What a life. Will I ever get back into the rat race at home? I hope not!

Then I had lunch with Ed Prewitt IV. I had dreaded this. Not dread, just wasn't looking forward to it. My duty for proud grandparents and friends, Ed and Irene. Well, surprise! He was a delightful young man—open, casual, easy, committed, knowing much about the city. I liked him. We had a long, good lunch.

And then I messed around this afternoon until early supper at Cafe Des Artistes with our dear friend Elvira and her friend Suzie. She had called from Atlanta and invited us earlier in the week. It was a delightful place, but real expensive! I paid before Elvira got the check—$170! I should have waited, but my male pride (or is it my sexism?) got the best of me, feeling that I need to be taking care of the women.

Then to the play, *M. Butterfly*. I had a hard time keeping my eyes open during acts one and two—too little sleep and too much wine. But then act three woke me up! It was powerful: loud and charged and moving, male/female, east/west, sexuality and politics. And it explored sex roles. (The mistress of twenty years turns out to be a man!)

Even with the power of that play, I'm beginning to get tired of the theater. For the first time in my whole life, I think I've seen enough. I think I've been stimulated enough. I'm glad not to see any other plays this week. Concerts are still not boring. But plays? I've gotten... not exactly bored... just used to them. Accustomed to them. And I don't like that. I don't want to become New York blasé.

Morning Run

I noted yesterday the peculiar relationship between the model in my painting class and the class. I looked at him for three classes—nine hours—very carefully studying the details of light on his skin, the unique curves in the muscles of his back. There he is naked and vulnerable. And yet, when he leaves the class, he does not even say good bye. As the professor (Dr. Tony) is leading a critique, the model simply puts his clothes on behind the screen and quietly slips away forever. I never even knew his name. And on the canvas, I'll carry a bit of him home. I know his body, but not his story or his name.

A great sadness—not depression—hit me on the way to school this morning on the subway. It was about leaving New York, about leaving this life and going back. It was an enormous sadness that weighed heavily—very heavily. I tried to shake it off. But the truth is . . . there is not much time left, and then it's home to Atlanta. Will Atlanta ever be home again in the same way? Probably not. Never, never the same.

I really do feel at home in New York. It's all so comfortable. I feel in charge, and not alien. I'm not impotent or at the mercy of city demons. I am grateful for that. I'm glad to feel at home.

FRIDAY

This morning I ran over the Brooklyn Bridge. What a treat! What a view! Going up is fairly steep, but not so much on the Brooklyn side. Coming down was fast and easy and exhilarating. It's still hard for me to believe when I run over the Brooklyn Bridge that I'm really here. Wow!

Yesterday's painting class was not satisfying. I just couldn't make it work. This painting is anemic—not powerful, like the first one. I tried too hard with the damn model's back. How can a back be interesting? I worked hard, but somehow the painting just didn't work very well.

It was a casual afternoon. David Seltzer, the writer/director of *Punchline* was at class last night. He was delightful. So very honest, so anti-establishment, so willing to risk. He's very hurt over *Punchline*'s reviews, and he doesn't like Sally Field. I think it's the best movie that we've seen. Billy Crystal was at Wednesday's class and we are sorry we missed him.

It strikes me that the more comfortable I feel here, the less profound my writing is, because my eyes get blind. I don't see as well when things are familiar. It's amazing how quickly things become familiar, and I don't see the mysteries or the depths or the anti-structure, or even God.

Maybe God is primarily experienced when things are not familiar, not controlled, not ordered, not comfortable. Perhaps God becomes a reality for us in the "gaps" of our experience, when the routine ongoingness of getting by seems to stop, when our ready roles disappear, when it's cold out and lonely in, and our fragility and potential nothingness become consciously available to us. When the disorder in the social order—crime, homelessness, sexual perversity, violence—raises its head and we are compelled to look or better yet, to see. Then God, or the lack of God, or the absence of God becomes very real indeed.

We can't bear the gaps very long. We "cover our eyes," "turn our backs," and get on with the routine of living. But if we don't occasionally face into the gaps, not only do we fearfully lack integrity, but we miss the Divine in the Depths, which may be the only place the Holy Other becomes accessible.

That must be why in ancient times all the great mystics and prophets, including Jesus, spent time in the desert. It was a significant "gap," not safe and ordered like the city was in those days. The desert was the place to wrestle with the demons and the angels.

Morning Run

    Maybe that is what Sondheim means by going "into the woods." To encounter the Holy Terror. Fearfully, but courageously, to face the giants and the witches in the gaps.

    Maybe it's all reversed nowadays. Maybe it's the city that has become the desert. Maybe it's the city that has become the place to struggle with what really matters in the ultimate sense. Maybe it's the city's chaotic bowels that are symbolically the place we have to venture for our trial—not the desert.

    One thing is certain; if we always stay with our own and in the comfortable routine of custom, whether at home or elsewhere, we never really come to the desert. An urban training retreat center could offer structured, middle-class, role-involved folk the opportunity to enter a gap—to walk toward the anti-structure—to go to the desert intentionally, trusting ultimately that the Holy is also the Just and the Good and the True.

SATURDAY

A nice, relaxing, comfortable, wonderful Saturday morning! Will I ever be able to leave this place? Going down for the paper, seeing the leaves spread out on the washed street, the guy at the newsstand says, "Not jogging this morning?" "No, it's Saturday; it's my day off!" A smile. The sun dabbles down on the street and on me. The sun is smiling too.

    Lying around reading the *Times* is so nice and easy. Gladness invades my heart. Simply experiencing the now. "Simply" is the key.

    Yesterday I did absolutely nothing for the first time in a long, long time. I felt tired, not sick-tired, just exhausted. I went to bed early. Today I feel good down to my bones, just good. "God's in his heaven, all's right with"... I hesitate... but not quite right. As I look up at the sun jutting down through the tall windows in the

November

apartment, I notice they really do need washing—all's not right, but today most all, anyway, is right with God's world.

MONDAY

Today, I ran over the Brooklyn Bridge again. It is such a thrill. Even though it was windy and freezing on the top of the Bridge, it was not really uncomfortable. Felix, my best friend, just called. He and his wife, Isabelle, will come over and we'll put them on an airplane for home at noon.

We had lunch yesterday with Ann and Ellen from Atlanta and Jule, an Alabama friend who now lives in New York, at the Village Green on Hudson Street. It was a beautiful clear day. Sunday, autumn air, everyone on the streets in the Village. When we came up from the subway station, people were handing out Dukakis buttons. We each got one and wore them proudly as we walked to the restaurant. It was a lovely, entertaining, and long lunch. We didn't leave until 2:30!

Dinner last night with Dick and Georgia in our building was very nice as well. He's head of social services at St. Margaret's House. We are not alone—we are here—there are others in this building who know and like us. There are others in this building who know our names. There is a community of sorts. What a change from when we first arrived.

This life we're living has such a nice rhythm. It scares me to be getting so accustomed to it.

WEDNESDAY

I don't know why I didn't write yesterday. Just forgot, I guess. I was certainly not overworked. Yesterday we went to the Guggenheim Museum—modern art—including a special Andy Warhol exhibit on cars. It was all very tacky to me, not moving at all, rather depressing.

Morning Run

The election yesterday was disappointing as well, even though it was expected. I'm bored with it; I'm bored with talking about it to myself or Allison. It's time to get on with something else.

Dinner last night with Bill was interesting, hearing about his new job with the National Episcopal Church, catching up with each other, reminiscing about old times and people. We got rather mellow—me on wine, Bill on scotch, Allison on Perrier (if that's possible!), and all three of us on each other.

I really love Bill and am beholden to him for so much. Rather than my father-in-God, as bishops are often called, he's been my big brother. And yet I find my reaction to him peculiar sometimes. A very important part of me is like him; we both grew up in church youth programs and were formed and defined by those wonderful green and sunny days at Camp McDowell, the diocesan camp. But when he talks about Camp McDowell and the comings and goings of the church in Alabama now, I feel my stomach become hollow—a certain emptiness. There's so much of my significant past connected with that youthful experience. It is what shaped me—gave me an agenda for my life. And yet that shaping place has left my life for good. Like the Tuscaloosa house I was reared in on Dearing Place, I'll never be in and out of there regularly or profoundly again.

That emptiness is not just the sweet pain of nostalgia. It's more the pain of a prophet not being honored in his own country or the painful truth of Thomas Wolfe's, "You can't go home again." It's probably weirdly connected with my feelings of not being appreciated or affirmed by Papa, which brings an added dimension of pain.

Also, I ask myself why Bill was hailed at home and stayed there for a long time with appreciation and grace and I did not. The name of that demon is envy!

November

All in all, Bill probably represents things in my past which both affirm me (those loving, graceful McDowell days) and at the same time things which disappoint and reject me. Add to all this what we lifelong Episcopalians feel about the bishops being the church, and Bill becomes burdened with my "love-hate" relationship with the church as well. Will I ever be rid of this ambiguity? Probably not. God help me. In the meantime, I'll pour Bill another Scotch and myself another glass of wine, and we'll tell dirty jokes, exchange church gossip, laugh about ourselves, and talk a little about Jesus. Amen.

THURSDAY

Neil Simon's *Rumors* was a delightful farce—star-studded, with Ken Howard, Ron Liebman, Jessica Walter, et cetera. It was fluff, but very funny.

The class discussion after the play today, however, was from last week's play with the cast of *Checkmates*. It was Ruby Dee and Denzel Washington and Paul Winfield. They're wonderful actors. Celebrities seem so natural when you're up close to them. At least those of the calibre of these. Shirley MacLaine was the same way. I guess when one achieves that sort of notoriety, then one is not easily threatened, and becomes more natural.

Last evening with another Atlanta group, which included David and Beverly and Anita and Jim and Mary, was fun. Beverly and David are such good folks, fundamentally nice and generous. Yet somehow it all felt a little less than comfortable to me. I'm just not quite ready to be back with Buckhead yet. Will I ever really feel at home with parish folks again? I so easily can slip back into my "Papa stuff," where growing up I would do almost anything—positive or negative—in hopes of getting my father's attention, in hopes of being noticed by him. Sometimes I think I live in perpetual

Morning Run

adolescence, wanting to shock and make my place and be noticed, and yet not wanting to live with the consequences. I'm a fifty-three-year-old adolescent, facing life with that no-win stance. If I'm noticed for good or ill, then somehow I'll be appreciated and loved (or some such malarkey as that!). Damn! And again I say, Damn!

It's really not a bad day today, but I'm working myself into feeling bad. I hate bad days. But that's life. Some days are bad. There's no way around it. This body just doesn't function perfectly every day. I notice my joints creak more nowadays and that getting up to our fourth floor stoop leaves me breathless! But then the good days come along. And they are so much better. I never appreciated feeling good on a good day as I have over the last few years. Perhaps that's the way I felt as a young person, but wasn't consciously aware of it. Anyway, I love those good days now! Those clear, sunny, upbeat days. Good Lord, help me to live good days and tolerate bad days without despair, and keep me walking on the water with my eyes on you.

FRIDAY

Yesterday continued the bad feeling. I couldn't paint anything. I couldn't get the drawing of the new painting on the canvas. And I finally painted over everything that was there. Dr. Tony said I was impetuous. He is right; I am. I meandered home with head-down depression. Is it worth it, my adolescent self said? In this morning's light, I realize I'm grieving leaving. I'm fearful of going back.

When I got home at five o'clock, Maria, our dear friend, was here, but she immediately got on the phone with Birmingham. There are no long distance lines from the Plaza in the late afternoon, she said. She's a big business executive, with deals and power. And then all of us went paddling around the Seaport in the rain, and I couldn't get a taxi to the restaurant in the Village

November

before our movie class. We all got very wet, particularly me, since I brought an umbrella for the women. By this time I had had it! The day got worse. How is it that my inside psyche and the outside world, on some days, seem to work in tandem to mess me up? Everything then becomes a thorough mess! I go wrong, and things go wrong, in a vicious cycle. And it rained!

Anyway, Allison and Maria got lost on the way from the train to supper—all of two and a half blocks! In the process, I got wet again, soaking wet, after I changed clothes once at the apartment. Allison simply walked around the block past the restaurant, after I went ahead—in good southern gentleman fashion—to make sure we had a table. They got "lost" under their one umbrella. I began to think they were hurt or something. I went around the block again in a frantic search, again getting soaked. They finally showed up. My panic changed to anger. I was furious. I was enraged, though controlled, in good southern gentleman form. We'll never make it to the class on time, I thought. We had a quick Chinese dinner. Because of my controlled anger, I felt cut off, alienated, impotent.

It's comic this morning. Distance, in time, helps humor. In fact, I guess humor requires some distance. But yesterday, last night wasn't funny at all!

Again, I think what's operating in me is part fear and part grief. They feel almost exactly the same. I put so much into getting away for this sabbatical, and now I am fearful what will happen when it's over. What will happen next? What will I be like? What will it be like?

I said to Allison coming home last night, "I really need a church." I don't seem to have or to belong to a church. I'm not talking about an institution or an organization, but I guess at its fundamental level, I need a community. I need a community that knows me and I know it and we know each other's names.

I said to Maria last night that a mutual friend of ours and I belong to different churches. What I meant

Morning Run

was that somehow we'd gotten separated—there was too much distance between us. We don't see things the same way any more.

I am so parochial about All Saints', even though at table with some parishioners the other night, I thought, "Can I go back to these folks? Are we still in the same church?"

Sometimes I feel so out of it. I seem to spend my life feeling out of it. Out is my state of being in the world. I'm always out, not in. Everyone thinks I'm in. I look like I'm in, but I don't feel in. I feel out. Why is that? Is it just my sin? Or the state of sin in general?

How I long to be in and me. Maybe that's a description of grace—in and me, both at the same time. What I experience is one or the other, either in and not me, or out and me. It's like Paul said, "Miserable creature that I am, who can deliver me from this body of death?"

Last night at film class was Dan Petrie, the famous director, and Sacho Mitchell, a fetching young star in *Spike of Bensonhurst*, a terrible movie that we previewed last week. This weekend we see *Cocoon II*, with the original cast and directed by Petrie. He's the father of Donald, who wrote and directed *Mystic Pizza*.

SATURDAY

God, the sun is shining and I feel better—much better. Thanks. Thanks. My depression comes on like something physical, a black cloud that drops in and then, somehow, lifts.

I'm still wondering, however, about going home to the same thing. I'm beginning to get ready to leave here, at least to leave what I've been doing here. It's finally beginning to get to me. I'm getting a little bored, more or less. My tolerance for the slow pace and the routine is very low. But I'm not looking forward to going home to the "same ole same ole" at All Saints'.

November

But I don't know what I want to do differently. If only the entire staff would just keep on doing what they've been doing with me gone, and let my presence be an additive—an addition. I would certainly help out pastorally, but I would not get into the administrative treadmill. However, I'm sure my wonderful colleagues don't want that, and I probably don't want that either. Later, we'll talk about it.

SUNDAY

It was a pretty day yesterday, very laid back. *Cocoon II* was not very satisfying. It could have been. It was almost satisfying, but missed by not being quite logical enough for the audience to accept all the space fantasy, and also the characterizations lacked integrity and believable warmth. A long lunch at One Fifth with Giles, the wife of a former student, was very relaxing. Afterwards, we walked around Times Square, deciding not to go to the theater. We bought tickets to *Driving Miss Daisy* for next Tuesday night. We rode the subway home, and I painted. It was the first time that I've painted away from class. I finally redeemed the painted-over canvas from last Thursday. It made me feel so good to do it, to produce. Fecundity, that's what it is, fecundity, to be fruitful. I do need to be fruitful. And occasionally to be productive.

A leisurely Sunday morning, propped up on the pull-out sofa with the *New York Times*. I read a long article on post-modern architecture. The writer connected the movement with Reagan's obsession with appearances—a wallowing in nostalgia of the past, not learning from the past. It is a refusal, the article said, to incorporate the present, with no vision for the future! I think I've settled for post-modernism in general lately. Allison and I both get into comfort sometimes and no pain. I wonder if that is the state of our middle age? I notice that I don't particularly like change as much as I used to. Allison really never has liked change.

Morning Run

Have I given up, burned out or something like that? I do cynically dip into the past, and at times I'm not pulled onward by a vision of the future. At times I think I'm not turned on or excited about anything much. There is a sort of blandness or repetition in just about everything. No, no. There is very little excitement about the new. Have I become a post-modernist in life—in the church?

I guess I've got too much innate dissatisfaction with things in general to be a settled-in, satisfied, or even fundamentally cynical person. All of that would make me a true post-modernist. Every now and then I think with Ecclesiastes that, "there's nothing new under the sun," but it usually comes out of some sort of despair. I suppose it gets close to cynicism sometimes, but I'm not primarily cynical. I mostly get angry. Sometimes I fear I've become an angry man, and that's, for me, so unattractive, not what I long to be. What's underneath my anger? Could it be a post-modernist despair—no new vision—no new excitement? That's not all it is. That's too easy, but it has truth in it.

The article claims post-modernism contains three important dimensions: anger, cynicism, despair. Are they present in the culture? Are they present in me? On occasion. But are they really creative? *No*, emphatically no. And what of these other post-modern attributes?

Nostalgia? I'm not really nostalgic, well, a little bit! Greed? I certainly have some of that. Sentimentality? No, well I do have some of that. Maybe I fear that.

I must quit all this abstract reflection and go to church! There's something rather ironic in that. But, commitments are commitments. "Let the dead bury the dead," Jesus said.

LATE SUNDAY

Reading the obituaries in the *Times* makes me think the entire arts/design/creative community is being

November

wiped out by AIDS. It is devastating. It burns a hole in my stomach. It is truly a plague. Everywhere I'm reminded of this plague—the graphic ads on the subways with slick colored pictures showing the contents of a woman's purse—compact, lipstick, and a condom—with the words, "Don't go out without your rubbers." The billboards are everywhere—education attempts to control this demon. Education can't cast it out.

I have never encountered an entity in my life that seems so evil, a demon invading the human scene to cause destruction and despair and death. And it gets so mixed up with pure rage in me—the red-hot fire of anger at discrimination and hate against the most pitiful of folk—God's dying children, deserted by family, thrown out on the streets. Carted off to die like the cadavers in the medieval black wagons of death.

Technically the church has not accepted homosexuality, and that ambiguity nourishes the insidiousness of homophobia. However, there is absolutely no ambiguity about a ministry to persons with AIDS. It is the Gospel's injunction and imperative to hold up the suffering and the dying, to bind up the world's wounds.

Good Lord, deliver us all. Good Lord, make us one. Good Lord, help us—help me!

MONDAY

I had a wonderful run this morning on a bright, cool, crisp day. It's amazing how the weather and sleep affect my soul.

We had lunch with old Tennessee friends, Bob and Miriam, at a wonderful little restaurant in the Village, The Black Sheep. It was fun. There is some thin shield I always experience with Bob—he's there, but not quite there—not really accessible. He's comfortable to be with, but slightly distant. I keep wanting to give him a final goose, and say, "Oh, come off it!" But he already

Morning Run

seems off it. It's as though there were a thin, transparent, but hard plastic shield in front of him. You can see through it to him, but when you begin to try to touch, you hit the hard, clear plastic.

Allison and I talk a lot about the children not getting married. It's amazing how that theme slips into my meditations. I feel terribly empty when I think of them alone, going through life alone—without children—without a mate or a companion to help them make it through the night. God, I would hate that for them.

I don't think it's selfish, basically. Of course I'd like grandchildren. But that's not it at bottom. I am concerned for them—for their souls' health. Doing it, making it alone is just fearsome to me, because I've always had Allison. I've never really been alone.

I guess I feel guilty. Did I do something wrong while rearing them? What did we do that was wrong? Why don't they make commitments? Why don't they find somebody to love and to connect with and to commit to? I don't understand it. I could beat myself up trying to figure out what we did wrong. But the question really is what can I do now? Can I help us and them feel better about what could happen ... about going through life by themselves?

I wish I could get the statement of Gertrude Caldwell over in Lutheran Towers out of my mind. "The greatest mistake I ever made was never marrying," she said, all alone in a high rise apartment for the elderly. All alone. Completely by herself with no family, and really no friends left. God, I don't want that for our children. Please, dear God, please.

TUESDAY

Today is wonderful—warm and sunny and clear. Running three times a week or walking down to get the paper in the morning makes me come alive—it wakes me up! I love this place—I truly love this little piece of

November

real estate. It is very peculiar. It's certainly not the beauty of the architecture or any such thing like that. There's some sort of magic energy that infuses me just to be on the street.

Yesterday was so very calm and gentle and peaceful and unhurried. After attending to some household errands, I went to the seminary, stopping in shops in Chelsea after getting off the train. I browsed in the bookstore and spent a long time in the library. Later I had a massage in an interesting loft on Fourteenth Street in the Village, and then home. Just a nice, quiet day.

I told Jim and Eulalie goodbye today. That's a first—saying goodbye from New York. It's very sad, and it's somewhat scary. Even though today going home has some excitement to it. It's strange, but I want to see the place and people—not any particular persons, but the people, as though they are one entity. I'm curious about what has happened in the city and in our neighborhood, and that curiosity is stronger than a longing to see anybody.

I want to see the staff at the church, but I'm somewhat afraid too. Will they wish I had not come back? Will they question my value? After all, everything has gotten along just fine without me.

Well, today looks like another jewel. It's to the Met for a class and then to *Driving Miss Daisy* tonight.

WEDNESDAY

I am in love with this city! What is it? Something not quite rational, like love. As I was thinking while running this morning—there must be some primitive, unconscious thing that energizes me about this city. I remember my old dreams about being here—those "tickets-to-show" dreams. In those repetitive dreams, we always had tickets to a Broadway show but somehow we never got there. I remember dreaming about

Morning Run

coming to New York as a very little boy, enamored by the lure of Broadway—the glitz and the lights, the myth, the romance—"Come along and listen to the lullaby of Broadway." The reality is here, but underneath, is that little-boy-lure-from-the-picture-shows-in-the-past. That Betty Grable shine calls me on, activated by some mysterious dynamic way below rationality.

Do I hate to leave it? Yes! Last night as we came out of *Driving Miss Daisy*—off Broadway on Forty-second Street and were walking up to Broadway, I was suddenly overcome with sadness about leaving ... all this ... this music of the city night.

Driving Miss Daisy—written by an Atlantan about Atlanta—made me hungry to see Atlanta, what is happening, what has changed. We went to see the play dressed very casually—both of us in Reeboks—me with my hair in a pony tail, Allison in a sweatsuit. We ran into Wilma and Carol from St. Luke's in Mountain Brook, our first parish. It's a posh suburban place. They were dressed to the nines for the theater, naturally. I was peculiarly embarrassed at how we looked. It made we aware of how New York we've become. And how I do love the casualness and the great gifts of anonymity.

THURSDAY

Up early this morning about five o'clock after not much sleep. But I am really up. I have been up all day yesterday and last night. I'm not sure why. I have simply felt so good and excited. Perhaps about the kids coming for Thanksgiving. Perhaps about getting back home. For the first time, going home—being at home—has turned me on. That's very curious.

The musical comedy, *Legs Diamond* was big, brassy, and boring. It was embarrassingly bad. We met with the cast afterward, and they don't know how bad it is. It's being worked on daily, they say. But with Peter Allen starring in it, it will never make it. I believe it is the worst show I've ever seen on Broadway, or anywhere else for that matter.

An evening last night with an Atlanta colleague, Woody, was both stimulating and relaxing at the same time. We ate dinner at the Bridge Cafe and had an interesting conversation about the importance of the earth—nature, the collective, the community, as opposed to the individual. I agreed with him about that importance. The individual (or individualism) becomes arrogant and, to me, sinful. It destroys the whole. It is, of course, a matter of balance or perspective. It is a way of viewing things.

Psychology has made us even more individualistic. The basic question, you see, is not "How's your psyche?" but "How's your community? How's your harmony? How's your ecology? How's the collective? How's your relationship to the earth? How is your humus—your humility—your relationship to the dirt?" To honor the earth is to be aware of your oneness with it. Therefore, humus, humility, dust to dust!

The Mystery to me is that one discovers that one matters only by giving up the question, "Do I matter?" and by giving oneself away on behalf of all people and things everywhere. Jesus had something to say about that Mystery for sure, "You find your life by giving your life away."

John the Baptist says, "Don't say, I have Abraham as my father. God can raise up out of those rocks, children of Abraham." That seems to me a declaration and a denouncement of narrow-viewing (Hebrew eyes) and the implied encouragement of wide-viewing: not "children of Abraham, but out of these *rocks*, children of Abraham," not faith in a particular heritage, but by faithfulness to the whole—the world, the universe, the earth—the humus, the rocks.

There is freedom in self-identification with the community—with the world. I am Harry because of be-

Morning Run

ing what? A Pritchett? A southerner? A man? A priest? An American? No . . . no. I am Harry because I am an earthling . . . a child of God! Of course we can value our particular and peculiar heritage, but that heritage is no excuse for not putting a higher value in the one world. Can anybody ever know unless they already know? Can anyone understand, unless they already understand? Who knows?

But I do love Joseph Campbell's admonition to us preachers in Moyers' book: "Preachers err by trying to talk people into belief; better they reveal the radiance of their own discovery." I don't know if I've got any radiance, but I do know that I have lots of discoveries. And I hope I never give up the quest.

FRIDAY

This morning the run was spectacular. Moving up the Brooklyn Bridge in the dark, the skyline on fire with reds and pinks and roses, the Manhattan Bridge silhouetted black against it. The morning star was shining like a spotlight. The twinkling lights of a train on the basement level of the bridge going over and the cars with their lights on the top level. And the view back toward the Seaport and downtown skyline was like Oz—but rather than the Emerald City, it was the Ruby City. The pink blaze of dawn reflecting in the mirror glass of the skyscrapers, the last clarity of a half-full moon, the pink glistening rubies in the water.

In the middle of the bridge, facing the dawn, all alone—I yelled, I really yelled out loud—as loud as I could yell,"Thank you, Jesus! Thank you Jesus!" My heart was about to burst. I had to yell, I had to praise! What a magnificent sight, what a magnificent place! It feels like being in love. I am in love, with life, with God. I feel the abandonment of lovers . . . and I am devastated with gratitude!

November

Not much sleep last night, but I'm still up. I don't know why. I'm not worried or anxious, but I need a catch-up day.

The last art class yesterday was wonderfully creative, but sad. Sad that it was the last. I feel like it's the last day of camp, or the day before moving. It's peculiar, because it's not sadness about leaving particular people or individuals, but sadness about leaving the place, the group: the art class, the New School, the people of the city. I felt the same way leaving the film class last night.

Again, our guest in the film class was Daniel Petrie, the director of *Cocoon II*. Also, Sylvia Miles who was in *Spike of Bensonhurst* as well as *Midnight Cowboy, Crossing Delancey, Wall Street*, and lots of other films. She was absolutely delightful—funny, charming. She said she was called to be an actress when she was seven years old. She used the word "called." She compared being an actress to being a priest. What an absolutely fascinating woman.

God, I hate giving up this class. It's so stimulating. It's a disciplined connection with popular culture—the movies—and a way to meet fascinating and entertaining guests. Could it be possible to run a similar class (without the guests of course) in Atlanta? And perhaps focus on theological interpretations of movies?

Art class is a creative structure as well. I am sure I won't paint alone. But going to a class and having the stimulation of other students in the class community would keep me painting and disciplined. I may do that in Atlanta. I'll investigate classes at Atlanta College of Art when we return.

SATURDAY

Last night in the River Cafe in Brooklyn, looking back at the skyline in lower Manhattan to where we live, was mystifying. This charming little restaurant with the

Morning Run

spectacular view is snuggled underneath the stately bridge on a cobblestone street, located on a barge. We were with Ann and Earnie from Atlanta, and Nell and Bill. We looked at the view when we first came in and Bill said "Can you believe I live there?" "Ha, ha," we all laughed. But I was thinking to myself for the first time, "I do want to live here. I really do."

Dinner was good, beautifully presented food (even better to look at than to eat) but very fine indeed to consume. We felt a genuine interest from our companions in what we had been doing, but more energy in simply sharing and laughing and eating and drinking and soaking up the warmth of the place.

I had a nice long day yesterday, alone. Allison went to Westchester County to visit Rita, a person she met in her design class. I am aware of two important observations: first, how mobile and independent and fearless Allison has become. As I look back over these writings, I have not seemed to note her metamorphosis to her old self. She has left behind the urban fear that plagued us both when we first arrived and become genuinely interested in the city experience and in new friends she has made. She is far better than I at developing friendships. I am so dependent on her for that dimension of our relationship as a couple to the world. And second, I am aware of how I value and need and want my alone time—even without her. I need this so much more than she seems to. I know that I love being with her and I love being away from her, and the rhythm and balance of that is necessary for both of us.

SUNDAY

It's pouring rain this morning, one of those dark days when I'd prefer to stay inside all day! What was that sad song in the fifties about gloomy Sunday? Well, today's gloomy Sunday. We are to meet friends at Trinity later this morning, so I guess we'll paddle up Wall Street.

November

Last night we met our good Atlanta friends Sue and John at the famous New York Athletic Club. It was so mellow and quiet. I understand so much better why New Yorkers cherish their old clubs, their shelters from the city storm. Later we ate heavy continental cuisine in a tiny but elegant French restaurant where everybody on the staff knew them. They are always supportive and kind to us. How royally we are living lately, what with dinners and clubs and taxis, no less!

MONDAY

Last weekend was not the best in many ways. Terribly rainy and dark all weekend. Several Atlanta and Huntsville friends were here. It felt like they were demanding our time. Of course they were not. It felt like they were competing for a piece of us, but of course, they were not. That is simply not true, but it felt like that. Also we heard from the Martins, not wanting our time particularly, but our wanting time with them before we leave. They have been so hospitable to us. It's all very crowding.

The problem, it seems to me, is this: people don't really want to hear about our stay, even though they say they do, and no doubt think they should want to hear about it. But what they really want is to tell us what's been going on with them. I do want to hear about them, but I also want to talk about us. Ahhh. Sin is simply ubiquitous! Ultimately, I guess, we all want to talk about ourselves to people we believe want to hear us.

Perhaps that's why going back home is rather scary and produces some anxiety. Allison says she fears what people will want of us. Perhaps. They will expect us to be rested and ready to hear all about them—what they've done since we've been gone. Perhaps.

It's the ambiguity of the mama and daddy roles, I guess. The children desire to tell the parents what

Morning Run

they (the children) have been up to, their comings and goings, but they're not particularly interested in hearing from the parents about the parents' own lives. Somehow, I've never been a good daddy—the role doesn't fit my own childishness. I want people to listen to me as well as my listening to them.

We must remember not to put down Atlanta in any way with some sort of New York arrogance. We have been accused in the past of putting down Birmingham or Tuscaloosa because of our big-city Atlanta arrogance. Now it grows even worse when I find myself inclined to speak derogatorily about Atlanta's provincialism in view of New York's cosmopolitanism. And, of course, New York's preeminence. New Yorkers (are we becoming like them?) tend to put down tourists. I must not be overcome by that sort of snobbery. I hear myself speaking authoritatively about New York's world view, when I've been here all of three months! Speaking of arrogance! It's busting out all over!

On the other hand, I bet I know more than some folks who have lived here a lot longer than we have. I like to immerse myself in a city: the culture, the nuances of its life, the local paper. I like to get into the city's skin and know it from the inside out. I have done that here. The issue is as old as Jesus... of being in the place, but not of the place.

I went alone yesterday for the second time to *Into the Woods*, and somehow in some mysterious way, everything came together. I don't know *how*; I only know *that*. Like the blind man who is healed, all he could say to the Pharisees was, "I was blind, and now I see, but I don't know why or who did the healing."

The play got to my soul... the second time around, after countless listenings to the tape. It was as though I "saw" it for the first time. I sat by myself on the eighth row, and I wept and I wept, holding back sobs. I knew why I came into the woods for this sab-

November

batical. I know more about the woods. Sondheim killed
me softly with his songs. It was pure grace.

> No more questions,
> Please.
> No more tests.
> Comes the day you say, "What for?"
> Please—no more.
>
> They disappoint,
> They disappear,
> They die but they don't . . .
>
> No more feelings.
> Time to shut the door.
> Just—no more.
>
> Running away—let's do it,
> Free from the ties that bind.
> No more despair
> Or burdens to bear
> Out there in the yonder.
>
> Running away—go to it.
> Where did you have in mind?
> Have to take care:
> Unless there's a "where,"
> You'll only be wandering blind
> Just more questions.
> Different kind.
>
> Where are we to go?
> Where are we ever to go?
>
> Running away—we'll do it.
> Why sit around, resigned?
> Trouble is, son,
> the farther you run,
> The more you feel undefined

Morning Run

For what you have left undone
And, more, what you've left behind.

We disappoint,
We leave a mess,
We die but we don't . . .

We disappoint
In turn, I guess.
Forget, though, we won't . . .

Like father, like son.

. . .

Careful the things you say,
Children will listen.
Careful the things you do,
Children will see.
And learn.

Children may not obey,
But children will listen.
Children will look to you
For which way to turn,
To learn what to be.

Careful the wish you make,
Wishes are children.
Careful the path they take—
Wishes come true,
Not free.

Careful the spell you cast,
Not just on children.
Sometimes the spell may last
Past what you can see
And turn against you . . .

Careful the tale you tell.
That is the spell.
Children will listen . . .

. . .

November

Nothing's quite so clear now—
Feel you've lost your way?
You are not alone,
Believe me.
No one is alone.
Truly . . .

You move just a finger,
Say the slightest word,
Something's bound to linger,
Be heard.
No one acts alone.
Careful, no one is alone.
People make mistakes.
Fathers, Mothers,
People make mistakes,
Holding to their own,
Thinking they're alone.
Honor their mistakes . . .
Everybody makes—
One another's
Terrible mistakes.
Witches can be right,
Giants can be good.
You decide what's right,
You decide what's good.

Just remember:
Someone is on your side.
Someone else is not.
While we're seeing our side—
Maybe we forgot:
They are not alone.
No one is alone.

Sometimes people leave you
Halfway through the woods.

Do not let it grieve you.
No one leaves for good.
No one is alone.

Morning Run

Things will come out right now.
We can make it so.
Someone is on your side,
No one is alone.
 . . .

Though it's fearful,
Though it's deep, though it's dark
And though you may lose the path,
Though you may encounter wolves,
You can't just act,
You have to listen.
You can't just act,
You have to think.

So it's
Into the woods
You go again,
You have to
Every now and then.
Into the woods,
No telling when,
Be ready for the journey.
Into the woods,
But not too fast
Or what you wish
You lose at last.

Into the woods, but mind the past.
Into the woods, but mind the future.
Into the woods, but not to stray,
Or tempt the Wolf or steal from the Giant—

The way is dark,
The light is dim . . .
But everything you learn there
Will help when you return there.

Into the woods—
You have to grope,

But that's the way
You learn to cope.
Into the woods
To find there's hope
Of getting through the journey.
Into the woods—
Each time you go,
There's more to learn
Of what you know.

"Amen" I said outloud on the subway heading back home, still red-eyed. And again I say "Amen Amen!"

I love being alone, but not alone. No one is alone. Going to the theater by myself, weeping, not caring who sees; I love the anonymity. Could I bear it for very long? I doubt it. But occasionally it is a God-send; literally, a God-send. In any sort of retreat program in the city, we must help people learn how to enjoy being alone in the city. We must help them to go "into the woods" in the city, to be renewed by that experience, rather than fearful of it.

TUESDAY

This morning as I opened the door from the street, I heard the nuns' soprano voices singing that ethereal soprano angel sound. What a lift—a gift—a grace. But ... ah ... what inconsistency. What incoherence ... what an anachronism, but what beauty and faith and truth and "just-rightness."

Last night with Dan and Deaner was warm and comfortable. We've known them for years. He's the rector of Trinity Church. Their apartment is enormous and absolutely beautiful—full of fine and elegant furniture and appointments and paintings and sculpture. Dinner

Morning Run

was lovely. They seem so pleased and right for New York. Theirs is one of those few situations in the church in which job and challenge and personal gifts have come together in a happy union. When that occurs, it is always grace.

WEDNESDAY

I hate endings; I hate last times. The last time to be in class, the last time at the Met, the last time at the market, the last time to go to the theater. All the omegas. I like alphas, not omegas.

As we left the Georgia O'Keeffe exhibition yesterday at the Met, we went by the Egyptian tomb where we started the history class on the first day. Ah, the beginnings and endings are coming together in a nice gestalt.

Tonight we'll go back to *Les Miserables*, the first play, I think. It's been so long, I can't remember. Now, the last play. Ah, sweet drama.

Margaret came in town yesterday. She and Allison went to *Phantom* last night. She is so beautiful and so smart and so aware of herself. She has so much imagination, independence, and just plain spunk. I love her so dearly.

Doug came in today—a little while ago, in fact. He is so lovely. He is so keenly sensitive as always, like he was even as a little boy. So fresh. His smile could light up the whole city!

Sonny comes soon. What a joy he is. He has become my friend, as well as my son. And to some degree I guess he always has been my friend. How blessed Allison and I are. Truly blessed with magnificent children, the good life, our health, and prosperity. And most of all, each other. How peculiar in the midst of the Mystery, that Allison and I found each other. How truly blessed—the alpha and the omega coming together in one. Surely, if beginnings bring the Mystery, so will the

November

end—the firsts *and* the lasts—will be full of the Mystery.

And Jesus said, "I am the alpha and the omega." This morning I do believe him. I really do.

FRIDAY

The Macy's Thanksgiving Day parade is traditional Americana, and we were in the middle of it yesterday. It was a clear, very cold day—the air cluttered with nothing but balloons and sunshine.

All of us went, riding the subway to Times Square. What a crowd—thousands and thousands. Children on daddies' shoulders, people standing on small stepladders. The crowd was like a swimming pool and we dove in, jumping occasionally to the surface to see what we could see. Sonny was taking pictures everywhere. Allison got a little claustrophobic. But overall it was an invigorating day. It all had a peculiar small-town air to it: rosy-cheeked, freckled-faced, middle American, clean. No sophistication, no subtlety, no depth, no real beauty. (Can eight-stories-high Bullwinkle balloons be aesthetically pleasing?) But it was fun, simple, pure, unpretentious. I loved it! My soul today feels as uncluttered and cleared out as the winter air.

Alleluia!!

SATURDAY

It's fun to have the children around. They are pleasant. Though they are always around when they're around. I look forward so desperately to their coming, and then I am always glad when they go home. Allison and I will have a day left alone before leaving here for good.

What is it about the children? Perhaps they just mess up my space. Perhaps they assume Allison is here in the world to please them, to wait on them. Perhaps I get childishly jealous after a while that Allison pays them so much attention. I don't know. I'll just be glad when they're gone. I long for them to come and see

Morning Run

them with excitement and glee, and then I'm always delighted when they depart.

Particularly this time, I'm needing to be alone. With all the goodbyes that I want to make—to places and things. That is so terribly peculiar; it's not goodbye to particular people, but to the place—the people collectively, like on the streets. Goodbye to this unique experience. That's what I desire to do alone.

This morning, before daybreak, at 5:45, Allison and I walked over Brooklyn Bridge together. We watched the sun come up over the Manhattan Bridge, set ablaze the glass towers of downtown—our neighborhood, we called it. We were all alone. It was clear and chilly but not too cold. It was so full . . . so life giving. But now it is goodbye to daybreak on the bridge together. And that is sad.

I really am a sentimental slob at heart! My inner life is that of a little boy. Perhaps it will always be that way. Sometimes I wish that my inner life would somehow grow up, but that's not what I seem to have inside.

SUNDAY

The last run. Hot, muggy morning. No one—almost no one—on the streets. Alone, but not at all lonely. All my old things and places, all telling me goodbye. In the mist, I'd swear Lady Liberty waved. Battery Park and Battery Park City—wow! What forlorn goodbyes. Folks sleeping in the doorways and benches at the park. A carload of young punks just ending their evening, and I think I hear them say as I run by, "Let's get him." And I speed up frantically to Broadway. The Court House, the Nathan Hale statue, George Washington at St. Paul's after his inauguration—goodbye. It's been so nice knowing you in the early mornings. Mauve, rose, purple clouds over Brooklyn Bridge. Twinkling tiny lights of the giant singing Christmas tree at the Seaport. The Indian guy down at the dock, where he's been

November

every morning since September with his legs crossed, palms up, facing the dawn in the East. My good friend, and we never said a word . . . but goodbye. Goodbye to my morning brother, on the last run.

The last run—is that a proper metaphor for our country? Is that a proper metaphor for New York City? The last run, running by Hale and Washington and Lady Liberty's welcome. The monument to Vietnam soldiers, the giant monument to the sailors killed in the wars, all the statues of all sorts of folk in the park. Running by long and narrow Wall Street, headed by a black, dark church. Running by all those monuments to the past—our past—our country's past, our past. And John the Baptist yells, "Don't say, 'Abraham was our father.' Out of these stones I can make sons of Abraham . . . The ax is at the trunk of the tree." Is it? Is it the last run?

Running by—running by. "But what shall we do?" the people asked John the Baptist? And he says, "Sell, give, don't cheat, be fair . . . maybe it won't be the end."

In the face of our country's apocalyptic last run, what shall we do? Whatever shall we do?

And is the last run a metaphor for the church in the 80s? Is this the last run for the church? Is the church living in the illusion of the run . . . the illusion that we're really getting somewhere but ending up after the run exactly where we started? Is it just good exercise? A work-out?

So what of that wonderful Mystery? That bride of Christ? That crazy anachronism so concerned now with Emily Post fussiness about liturgical niceties, that effete laziness of prissy priesthood. That out-of-shape body of Christ, arrogantly assuming the city or the country cares about theological fine points, cares about what we do and when we meet, and all the political shenanigans of yuppie Christendom. Ah, the illusions of the last run. Out of these stones—the stones of the city streets—God will make children of Abraham! God will

Morning Run

make God's own faithful people, who go out, like Abraham, not knowing exactly where they're going, but in faith running toward the Promised Land!

But it is *my* last run today. The last run in the city. It's a soaking, steady rain now—still warm. Through the Seaport, clouds over the water and the Brooklyn Bridge. I run under the FDR Highway all the way up, past the Manhattan and the Queensboro Bridges. And in the yellowing mist I don't pass one single runner. I begin to think as I run, I am really ready to go home. I'm ready to be on my way. All the children have gone. Allison and I will go out for the last supper tonight, after getting everything ready today. We had the last brunch at the Black Sheep in the Village yesterday, and I did so hate to leave that place. But still and all, I am ready today. I am ready to go home.

The last run may not be this city's, nor our country's, nor the church's basic metaphor, but the run is *my* primary metaphor—the morning run—it is a metaphor for my life. As I reached Fulton Street a little while ago, I heard Malcolm Boyd's voice yelling again, "Are you running with me, Jesus?"

And I joined in the chorus. Are you running with me, Jesus? Are you running with us, Jesus? It is the autumn of my life and it is the morning of my life, and I am on the run. Are you running with me, Jesus?

Most of all, as I open the door to climb up to the fourth floor, I am aware of being bathed in thanksgiving. Literally wallowing in my overflowing thanks. My deepest thanks, for a blessed life—for a lovely, once in a lifetime experience, and for knowing in my heart of hearts, that without Jesus, there would be no one to thank for the mornings and no one to be my companion on the morning run.

THE AUTHOR

The Reverend Doctor Harry H. Pritchett, Jr. is Rector of All Saints' Church, a large and lively multifaceted parish in downtown Atlanta. Before assuming this position in 1981, he was Archdeacon of the Episcopal Diocese of Alabama.

Mr. Pritchett has led conferences, retreats, and consultations for clergy and laity throughout the United States. Although his fields of interest are varied, he focuses on parish development, education, and spiritual growth. He has contributed to several books in the area of parish development and theological reflection. He is the author of *God is a Surprise Songbook,* Creative Material Library, and the originator of the frequently published *The Story of Phillip.* He has contributed articles and sermons to national publications of the Episcopal, Lutheran, Roman Catholic, Methodist, Presbyterian, and Baptist churches.

Mr. Pritchett holds a M.Div. degree from Virginia Theological Seminary and a D.D. degree from Centre College. He has served parishes in the Diocese of Alabama and was Director of Parish Field Education on the faculty of the School of Theology, Sewanee, Tennessee.